HAPPY BAKING

Love from

grandad & gran xx

special cakes

essential recipes

Publisher's Note:
Raw or semi-cooked eggs should not be consumed by babies, toddlers,
pregnant or breastfeeding women, the elderly or those suffering from a chronic illness.

Publisher & Creative Director: Nick Wells
Senior Project Editor: Catherine Taylor
Art Director: Mike Spender
Layout Design: Jane Ashley
Digital Design & Production: Chris Herbert
Proofreader: Dawn Laker

Special thanks to Alex McClean, Laura Zats and Laura Bulbeck.

This is a **FLAME TREE** book
FLAME TREE PUBLISHING
Crabtree Hall, Crabtree Lane
Fulham, London SW6 6TY
United Kingdom
www.flametreepublishing.com

Flame Tree is part of The Foundry Creative Media Company Limited

First published 2012

A copy of the CIP data for this book is available from the British Library.

Printed in China

special cakes

essential recipes

General Editor: Gina Steer

**FLAME TREE
PUBLISHING**

Contents

Equipment & Utensils

Cooking equipment not only assists in the kitchen, but can make all the difference between success and failure. Take the humble cake tin; although a very basic piece of cooking equipment, it plays an essential role in baking. Using a tin that is too large will spread the mixture too thinly and the result will be a flat, limp-looking cake. On the other hand, cramming the mixture into a tin which is too small will result in the mixture rising up and out of the tin.

Bakeware

To ensure successful baking, it is worth investing in a selection of high-quality tins, which, if looked after properly, should last for many years. Follow the manufacturer's instructions when first using and ensure that the tins are thoroughly washed and dried after use and before putting away.

Sandwich Cake Tins

Perhaps the most useful of tins for baking are sandwich cake tins, ideal for classics such as Victoria sponge cake. You will need two tins and they are normally 18 cm/7 inches or 20.5 cm/8 inches in diameter and are about 5–7.5 cm/2–3 inches deep and often nonstick.

Deep Cake Tins

With deep cake tins, it is personal choice whether you buy round or square tins. They vary in size from 12.5–35.5 cm

/5–14 inches with a depth of between 12.5–15 cm/5–6 inches. A deep cake tin, for everyday fruit or Madeira cake, is a must; a useful size is 20.5 cm/8 inches.

Loaf Tins

Loaf tins come in two sizes, 450 g/1 lb and 900 g/2 lb.

Other Tins

There are plenty of other tins to choose from, ranging from themed and shaped tins, such as Christmas trees, numbers and petals, to ring mould tins (tins with a hole in the centre) and springform tins, where the sides release after cooking, allowing the finished cake to be removed easily. A selection of different sized roasting tins is also a worthwhile investment, as they can double up as a bain-marie, or for cooking larger quantities of cakes such as gingerbread.

Other Essential Items

Mixing bowls

Three to four different sizes of mixing bowls are also very useful for mixing and melting ingredients.

Wire Cooling Racks

Another essential piece of equipment is a wire cooling rack. It is crucial when baking to allow cakes to cool after being removed from their tins. A wire rack also protects your kitchen surfaces from the heat and allows air to circulate around the goodies, speeding cooling and preventing soggy bottoms.

Measuring Items and Cutlery

Baking needs 100 per cent accuracy to ensure a perfect result. Scales come in many shapes and sizes, both digital and with weights. Most have a weigh pan although, with some, your own bowl is used. Measuring jugs and spoons are essential for accurate measuring of both dry and wet ingredients. Basic mixing cutlery is also essential, such as a wooden spoon (for mixing and creaming), a spatula (for transferring the mixture from the mixing bowl to the baking tins and spreading the mixture once it is in the tins) and a palette knife (to ease cakes out of their tins before placing them on the wire racks to

cool). Also, don't forget a fine-mesh sieve, for sifting flour and powders.

Electrical Equipment

Nowadays, help from time-saving gadgets and electrical equipment makes baking far easier and quicker. Equipment can be used for creaming, mixing, beating, whisking, grating and chopping. There is a wide choice of machines available from the most basic to the highly sophisticated.

Food Processors

First, decide what you need your processor to do when choosing a machine. If you are a novice to baking, it may be a waste to start with a machine which offers a wide range of implements and functions. This can be off-putting and result in not using the machine to its ultimate potential.

When buying a food processor, look for measurements on the side of the processor bowl and machines with a removable feed tube, which allows food or liquid to be added while the motor is still running. Look out for machines that have the facility to increase the capacity of the bowl and have a pulse button for controlled chopping. For many, storage is an issue, so reversible discs and flex storage, or on more advanced models, a blade storage compartment or box, can be advantageous.

It is also worth thinking about machines which offer optional extras which can be bought as your cooking requirements change. Mini chopping bowls are available for those wanting to chop small quantities of food. If time is an issue, dishwasher-friendly attachments may be vital. Citrus presses, liquidisers and whisks may all be useful attachments for the individual cook.

Blenders

Blenders often come as attachments to food processors and are generally used for liquidising and puréeing foods. There are two main types of blender. The first is known as a goblet blender. The blades of this blender are at the bottom of the goblet with measurements up the sides. The second blender is portable. It is handheld and should be placed in a bowl to blend.

Mixers

Table-top mixers are freestanding and are capable of dealing with fairly large quantities of mixture. They are robust machines and good for heavy cake mixing as well as whipping cream, whisking egg whites or making one-stage cakes. These mixers also offer a wide range of attachments ranging from liquidisers, mincers, juicers, can openers and many more and varied attachments.

Handheld mixers are smaller than freestanding mixers and often come with their own bowl and stand from which they can be lifted off and used as handheld devices. They have a motorised head with detachable twin whisks. These mixers are particularly versatile, as they do not need a specific bowl in which to whisk. Any suitable mixing bowl can be used.

Essential Ingredients

The quantities may differ, but basic baking ingredients do not vary greatly. Let us take a closer look at the baking ingredients which are essential.

Fat

Butter and margarine are the fats most commonly used in baking. Others that can be used include white vegetable fat, lard and oil. Low-fat spreads are not recommended for baking, as they break down when cooked at a high temperature. Often it is a matter of personal preference which fat you choose but there are a few guidelines that are important to remember.

Butter and Margarine

Unsalted butter is the fat most commonly used in cake making, especially in rich fruit cakes and the heavier sponge cakes such as Madeira or chocolate torte. Unsalted butter gives a distinctive flavour to the cake. Some people favour margarine, which imparts little or no flavour to the cake.

As a rule, butter and firm block margarine should not be used straight from the refrigerator but allowed to come to room temperature before using (allow about an hour to soften). Also, it should be beaten by itself first before creaming or rubbing in. Soft margarine is best suited to one-stage recipes.

Oil

Light oils, such as vegetable or sunflower, are sometimes used instead of solid fats. However, if oil is used, be careful – it is vital to follow a specific recipe because the proportions of oil to flour and eggs are different and these recipes will need extra raising agents.

Flour

We can buy a wide range of flours all designed for specific jobs. There is even a special sponge flour designed especially for whisked sponges. It is also possible to buy flours that cater for coeliacs, which contain no gluten. Buckwheat, soy and chickpea flours are also available. Flour can also come ready sifted.

Which Flour to Use

Strong flour, which is rich in gluten, whether it is white or brown (this includes granary and stoneground), is best kept for bread and Yorkshire pudding. Ordinary flour or weak flour is best for cakes, as it absorbs the fat easily and gives a soft light texture. This flour comes in plain white or self-raising, as well as wholemeal. Self-raising flour, which has the raising agent already incorporated, is best kept for sponge cakes, where it is important that an even rise is achieved.

Plain flour can be used for all types of baking. If using plain flour for cakes, unless otherwise stated in the recipe, use 1 teaspoon of baking powder to 225 g/8 oz of plain flour. With sponge cakes and light fruit cakes, it is best to use self-raising flour as the raising agent has already been added to the flour. This way, there is no danger of using too much which can result in a sunken cake with a sour taste.

Other Raising Agents

There are other raising agents that are also used. Some cakes use bicarbonate of soda with or without cream of tartar, blended with warm or sour milk. Whisked eggs also act as a raising agent as the air trapped in the egg ensures that the mixture rises. Generally, no other raising agent is required.

Eggs

There are many types of eggs sold and it really is a question of personal preference which ones are chosen. All offer the same nutritional benefits. Store eggs in the refrigerator with the round end uppermost and allow them to come to room temperature before using.

Sizes

When a recipe states 1 egg, it is generally accepted this refers to a medium egg. Over the past few years, the grading of eggs has changed. For years, eggs were sold as small, standard and large, then this method changed and they were graded in numbers with 1 being the largest. The general feeling by the public was that this system was misleading, so now we buy our eggs as small, medium and large.

Types

The majority of eggs sold in this country come from caged hens. These are the cheapest eggs and the hens have been fed on a manufactured mixed diet. Barn eggs are from hens kept in barns who are free to roam within the barn. However, their diet is similar to caged hens and the barns may be overcrowded.

Free-range eggs are from hens that lead a much more natural life and are fed natural foods. This, however, is not always the case and in some instances they may still live in a crowded environment and fed the same foods as caged and barn hens. Organic eggs are from hens that live in a flock, whose beaks are not clipped and who are completely free to roam. Obviously, these eggs are much more expensive than the others.

Safety

Due to the slight risk of salmonella, all eggs are now sold date stamped to ensure that the eggs are used in their prime. This applies even to farm eggs which are no longer allowed to be sold straight from the farm. Look for the lion quality stamp (on 75 per cent of all eggs sold) which guarantees that the eggs come from hens vaccinated against salmonella, have been laid in the UK and are produced to the highest food safety standards. All of these eggs carry a best-before date. Do remember that raw or semi-cooked eggs should not be given to babies, toddlers, pregnant women, the elderly and those suffering from a recurring illness.

Sugar

Sugar not only offers taste to baking but also adds texture and volume to the mixture. It is generally accepted that caster sugar is best for sponge cakes. Its fine granules disperse evenly when creaming or whisking. Granulated sugar is used for more general cooking, such as stewing fruit, whereas demerara sugar with its toffee taste and crunchy texture is good for sticky puddings and cakes. For rich fruit cakes, Christmas puddings and cakes, use the muscovado sugars which give a rich intense treacle flavour. Icing sugar is used primarily for icings and can be used in fruit sauces when the sugar needs to dissolve quickly.

Working with Chocolate

Chocolate can be used in cakes to create flavour and colour, as well as to decorate. Who can resist its charms?

Melting Chocolate

As a general rule, it is important not to allow any water to come into contact with the chocolate. In fact, a drop or two of water is more problematic than larger amounts, which may blend in. The melted chocolate will 'seize' (turn into a grainy, clumpy mess) and it will be impossible to bring it back to a smooth consistency.

Do not overheat chocolate or melt it by itself in a pan over a direct heat. Always use either a double boiler or a heatproof bowl set over a saucepan of water, but do not allow the bottom of the bowl to come into contact with the water. Check the chocolate every couple of minutes, reducing or extinguishing the heat under the saucepan as necessary. Stir the chocolate once or twice during melting until it is smooth and no lumps remain. Do not cover the bowl once the chocolate has melted or condensation will form, water will drop into it and it will be ruined.

Microwaving is another way of melting chocolate, but again, caution is required. Follow the oven manufacturer's instructions together with the instructions on the chocolate and proceed with care. Melt the chocolate in bursts of 30–60 seconds, stirring well between bursts, until the chocolate is smooth. If possible, stop microwaving before all the chocolate has melted and allow the residual heat in the chocolate to finish the job.

Making Chocolate Decorations

There are a few useful techniques for working with chocolate. None of them is very complicated, and a can be mastered easily with a little practice.

Curls

To make curls, melt the chocolate following your preferred method and then spread it in a thin layer over a cool surface, such as a marble slab, ceramic tile or piece of granite. Leave until just set but not hard. Take a clean paint scraper or cheese plane and set it at an angle to the surface of the chocolate, then push, taking a layer off the surface. This will curl until you release the pressure.

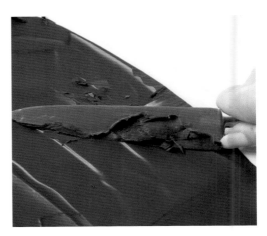

Caraque

Caraque are long thin curls. To make caraque, prepare the chocolate in the same way as for the curls. Use a large sharp knife and hold it at about a 45–degree angle to the chocolate. Hold the handle and the tip and scrape the knife towards you, pulling the handle but keeping the tip more or less in the same place. This method makes thinner, tighter, longer curls.

Shaved and Grated Chocolate

Using a vegetable peeler, shave a thick block of chocolate to make mini curls or use a sharp long–bladed knife to make big shavings. These are best achieved if the chocolate is a little soft, otherwise it has a tendency to break into little flakes. Or use a grater to achieve even tinier shavings.

Chocolate Shapes

Spread a thin layer of chocolate, as described in the instructions for chocolate curls, and allow to set as before. Use shaped cutters or a sharp knife to cut out shapes. Use to decorate your cakes.

Chocolate Modelling Paste

To make chocolate modelling paste (very useful for cake coverings and for making heavier shapes, such as ribbons) put 200 g/7 oz plain chocolate in a bowl and add 3 tablespoons of liquid glucose. Set the bowl over a pan of gently simmering water. Stir until the chocolate is just melted, then remove from the heat. Beat until smooth and leave the mixture to cool. When cool enough to handle, knead to a smooth paste on a clean work surface. The mixture can now be rolled and cut to shape. If the paste hardens, wrap it in clingfilm and warm it in the microwave for a few seconds on low.

Basic Methods

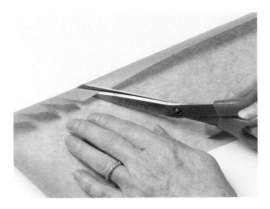

Lining

If a recipe states that the tin needs lining, do not be tempted to ignore this. Rich fruit cakes and other cakes that take a long time to cook benefit from the tin being lined so that the edges and base do not burn or dry out.

Papers

Greaseproof paper or baking parchment is ideal for this. It is a good idea to have the paper at least double thickness, or preferably three to four layers. Sponge cakes and other cakes that are cooked in 30 minutes or less are also better

if the bases are lined, as it is far easier to remove them from the tin.

Technique

The best way to line a round or square tin is to draw lightly around the base and then cut just inside the markings, making it easy to sit in the tin. Next, lightly oil the paper so it peels away easily from the cake. If the sides of the tin also need to be lined, then cut a strip of paper long enough for the tin. This can be measured by wrapping a piece of string around the rim of the tin. Once again, lightly oil the paper, push against the tin and oil once more, as this will hold the paper to the sides of the tin.

Separating Eggs

When separating eggs (that is, separating the white from the yolk), crack an egg in half lightly and cleanly over a bowl, being careful not to break the yolk and keeping it in the shell. Then tip the yolk backwards and forwards between the two shell halves, allowing as much of the white as possible to spill out into the bowl. Keep or discard the yolk and/or the white as needed. Make sure that you do not get any yolk in your whites, as this will prevent successful whisking of the whites. It takes practice!

Different Mixing Techniques

Creaming

The creaming method – which means that the butter and sugar are first beaten or 'creamed' together – makes light cakes. A little care is needed for this method. Use a large mixing bowl to beat the fat and sugar together until pale and fluffy. The eggs are gradually beaten in to form a slackened batter and the flour is folded in last, to stiffen up the mixture.

Rubbing In

In this method, the fat is lightly worked into the flour between the fingers, as in pastry-making, until the mixture resembles fine crumbs. This can be done by hand or in a

food processor. Enough liquid is stirred in to give a soft mixture that will drop easily from a spoon. This method is used for easy fruit cakes.

All-In-One Mixtures

This 'one-stage' method is quick and easy and is perfect for those new to baking, as it does not involve any complicated techniques. It is ideal for making light sponges, but soft tub-type margarine or softened butter at room temperature must be used. All the ingredients are simply placed in a large bowl and quickly beaten together for just a few minutes until smooth. Be careful not to overbeat, as this will make the mixture too wet. Self-raising flour with the addition of a little extra baking powder is vital for a good rise.

The Melting Method

Cakes with a delicious moist sticky texture, such as gingerbread, are made by this method. These cakes use a high proportion of sugar and syrup, which are gently warmed together in a saucepan with the fat, until the sugar has dissolved and the mixture is liquid. It is important to cool the hot melted mixture a little before beating in flour, eggs and spices to make the batter, otherwise it will damage the power of the raising agent.

Icing Recipes

Cream Cheese Frosting

Covers a 20 cm/8 in round cake or 12 cupcakes

50 g/2 oz unsalted butter, softened
300 g/11 oz icing sugar, sifted
flavouring of choice
food colourings
125 g/4 oz cream cheese

Beat the butter and icing sugar together until light and fluffy. Add the flavourings and colourings of choice and beat again. Add the cream cheese and whisk until light and fluffy. Do not overbeat, however, or the mixture can become runny.

Basic Buttercream

Covers a 20 cm/8 in round cake or 12 cupcakes

150 g/5 oz unsalted butter, softened
225 g/8 oz icing sugar, sifted
2 tbsp hot milk or water
1 tsp vanilla extract
food colourings of choice

Beat the butter until light and fluffy, then beat in the sifted icing sugar and hot milk or water in two batches. Add the

vanilla extract and any food colourings. Store chilled for up to 2 days in a lidded container.

Royal Icing

Covers a 20 cm/8 in round cake or 12 cupcakes

2 medium egg whites
500 g/1 lb 1 oz icing sugar, sifted
2 tsp lemon juice

Put the egg whites in a large bowl and whisk lightly with a fork to break up the whites until foamy. Sift in half the icing sugar with the lemon juice and beat well with an electric mixer for 4 minutes, or by hand with a wooden spoon for about 10 minutes until smooth.

Gradually sift in the remaining icing sugar and beat again until thick, smooth and brilliant white and the icing forms soft peaks when flicked up with a spoon. Keep the royal icing covered with a clean damp cloth until you are ready to use it, or store in the refrigerator in a tightly lidded plastic container until needed. If making royal icing ahead of time to use later, beat it again before use to remove any air bubbles that may have formed in the mixture.

Glacé Icing

Covers a 20 cm/8 in round cake or 12 cupcakes

225 g/8 oz icing sugar
few drops lemon juice, or vanilla or almond extract
2–3 tbsp boiling water
liquid food colouring

Sift the icing sugar into a bowl and add the chosen

flavouring. Gradually stir in enough water to mix to a consistency of thick cream. Beat with a wooden spoon until the icing is thick enough to coat the back of the spoon. Add colouring, if liked, and use at once, because the icing will begin to form a skin.

Apricot Glaze

Covers two 20 cm/8 in round cakes or 24 cupcakes

450 g/1 lb apricot jam
3 tbsp water
1 tsp lemon juice

Place the jam, water and juice in a heavy-based saucepan and heat gently, stirring, until soft and melted. Boil rapidly for 1 minute, then press through a fine sieve with the back of a wooden spoon. Discard the pieces of fruit. Use immediately for glazing or sticking on almond paste and/or fondant, or pour into a clean jar or plastic container, seal and refrigerate for up to 3 months.

Almond Paste

Covers two 20 cm/8 in round cakes or 24 cupcakes

125 g/4 oz icing sugar, sifted
125 g/4 oz caster sugar
225 g/8 oz ground almonds
1 medium egg
1 tsp lemon juice

Stir the sugars and ground almonds together in a bowl. Whisk the egg and lemon juice together and mix into the dry ingredients. Knead until the paste is smooth. Wrap tightly in clingfilm or foil and store in the refrigerator until needed. The paste can be made 2–3 days ahead of time, but after that it will start to dry out and become difficult to handle.

To use the almond paste, knead on a surface lightly dusted with icing sugar until soft and pliable. Brush the top of each cake with apricot glaze. Roll out the paste and cut out discs to cover the tops of the cakes. Press onto the cakes.

Rolling Fondant (Sugarpaste)

Covers a 20 cm/8 in round cake or 12 cupcakes, or use for decorations

1 medium egg white
1 tbsp liquid glucose
350 g/12 oz icing sugar, sifted

Place the egg white and liquid glucose in a large mixing bowl and stir together with a fork, breaking up the egg white. Add the icing sugar gradually, mixing in with a palette knife, until the mixture binds together and forms a ball. Turn the ball of fondant out onto a clean surface dusted with icing sugar and knead for 5 minutes until soft but firm enough to roll out. If the icing is too soft, knead in a little more icing sugar until the mixture is pliable.

To colour, knead in paste food colouring. Do not use liquid food colouring, because this is not suitable and will make the fondant go limp.

To use, roll out thinly on a clean surface dusted with icing sugar and cut out discs or shapes to cover cakes, on top of almond paste or buttercream, if liked. Or mould into three-dimensional shapes and leave to dry for 24 hours in egg cartons lined with clingfilm.

Special Occasion Cakes

What two words go better together than cake and celebration? With the recipes in this section, you'll be taking your special occasion to the next level of indulgence. Feast on the lavish French Chocolate Pecan Torte and lose yourself in the superb flavours of the Buttery Passion Fruit Madeira Cake to make your day extra-special!

Christmas Cake

1 Place the dried fruit and cherries in a bowl and sprinkle over the brandy or orange juice and the lemon zest and juice. Stir and let soak for 2–4 hours. Preheat the oven to 150°C/300°F/Gas Mark 2. Grease and double-line the base and sides of a 20.5 cm/8 inch round deep cake tin. Beat the sugar and butter together until soft and fluffy. Beat the eggs in gradually, adding 1 teaspoon of flour with each addition. Stir in the treacle, then sift in the rest of the flour and the spice. Add the soaked fruit and stir until the mixture is smooth. Spoon into the tin and smooth the top level. Bake for 1 hour, then reduce the temperature to 140°C/275°F/Gas Mark 1 and bake for a further 2–2½ hours until a skewer inserted into the centre comes out clean. Leave the cake to cool in the tin, then, when completely cold, remove and wrap in greaseproof paper and then in foil and store in a cool place for 1–3 months.

2 To decorate, brush the cake all over with brandy, if using. Heat the jam and brush over the top and sides. Roll out one third of the almond paste and cut into a disc the size of the top of the cake, using the empty tin as a guide. Place the disc on top. Roll the remaining paste into a strip long enough to cover the sides of the cake and press on. Leave the almond paste to dry out in a cool place for 2 days. On a surface dusted with icing sugar, roll out the sugarpaste to a circle large enough to cover the top and sides of the cake. Brush 1 tablespoon brandy or cold boiled water over the almond paste and place the sugarpaste on top. Smooth down and trim. Make a border from tiny balls of sugarpaste and decorate.

Ingredients SERVES 12-14

900 g/2 lb mixed dried fruit
75 g/3 oz glacé cherries, rinsed
  and halved
3 tbsp brandy or orange juice
finely grated zest and juice of 1 lemon
225 g/8 oz soft dark muscovado sugar
225 g/8 oz butter, at room temperature
4 medium eggs, beaten
225 g/8 oz plain flour
1 tbsp black treacle
1 tbsp mixed spice

To decorate:

2–4 tbsp brandy (optional)
4 tbsp sieved apricot jam
700 g/1½ lb almond paste (see
  page 15)
icing sugar, for dusting
1 kg/2 lb 3 oz ready-to-roll sugarpaste
bought decorations and ribbon

Supreme Chocolate Gateau

1 Preheat the oven to 180°C/350°F/Gas Mark 4, 10 minutes before baking. Lightly oil and line three 20.5 cm/8 inch round tins. Whisk all the cake ingredients together until thick; add a little warm water if very thick. Spoon into the tins. Bake for 35–40 minutes until a skewer comes out clean. Cool on wire racks.

2 Very gently heat 2 tablespoons hot water with 50 g/2 oz of the chocolate and stir until combined. Remove from the heat and leave for 5 minutes. Place the gelatine into a dish and add 2 tablespoons cold water. Leave for 5 minutes, squeeze out any excess water and add to the chocolate. Stir until dissolved. Whip the cream until just thickened. Add the chocolate mixture and continue whisking until soft peaks form. Leave until starting to set. Place one of the cakes onto a plate and spread with half the cream mixture. Top with a second cake and the remaining cream, cover with the third cake and chill until the cream has set.

3 Melt 175 g/6 oz of the chocolate with the butter and stir until smooth; leave until thickened. Melt the remaining chocolate. Cut twelve 10 cm/4 inch squares of foil. Spread the chocolate evenly over them to within 2.5 cm/1 inch of the edges. Chill for 3–4 minutes until just set but not brittle. Gather up the corners and return to the refrigerator until firm. Spread the chocolate and butter mixture over the top and sides of the cake. Remove the foil from the curls and use to decorate the top of the cake. Dust with cocoa powder and serve cut into wedges.

Ingredients   SERVES 12–14

For the cake:
175 g/6 oz self-raising flour, sifted
1½ tsp baking powder, sifted
3 tbsp cocoa powder, sifted
175 g/6 oz margarine or
    butter, softened
175 g/6 oz caster sugar
3 large eggs

To decorate:
350 g/12 oz dark chocolate
1 gelatine leaf
200 ml/7 fl oz double cream
75 g/3 oz butter
cocoa powder, for dusting

Helpful Hint
If you prefer, make ordinary chocolate curls to decorate this cake.

Double Chocolate Cake with Cinnamon

1 Preheat the oven to 190°C/375°F/Gas Mark 5, 10 minutes before baking. Lightly oil and line the base of two 20.5 cm/8 inch sandwich tins with greaseproof paper or baking parchment. Sift the cocoa powder, cinnamon and flour together and reserve.

2 In a large bowl, cream the butter or margarine and sugar until light and fluffy. Beat in the eggs a little at a time until they are all incorporated and the mixture is smooth. (If it looks curdled at any point, beat in 1 tablespoon of the sifted flour.)

3 Using a rubber spatula or metal spoon, fold the sifted flour and cocoa powder into the egg mixture until mixed well. Divide between the two prepared cake tins and level the surface. Bake in the preheated oven for 25–30 minutes until springy to the touch and a skewer inserted into the centre of the cake comes out clean. Turn out onto a wire rack to cool.

4 To make the filling, coarsely break the white chocolate and heat the cream very gently in a small saucepan. Add the broken chocolate, stirring, until melted. Leave to cool, then, using half of the cooled white chocolate, sandwich the cakes together.

5 Top the cake with the remaining cooled white chocolate. Coarsely grate the dark chocolate over the top and serve.

Ingredients   SERVES 10

50 g/2 oz cocoa powder
1 tsp ground cinnamon
225 g/8 oz self–raising flour
225 g/8 oz unsalted butter or
   margarine
225 g/8 oz caster sugar
4 large eggs

For the filling:
125 g/4 oz white chocolate
50 ml/2 fl oz double cream
25 g/1 oz dark chocolate

Helpful Hint
Adding some sifted flour can help to prevent the mixture from curdling (see step 2). Removing the eggs from the refrigerator and allowing them to return to room temperature before use also helps. Remember to add just a little egg at a time!

3

4

Mother's Day Rose Cupcakes

1 Preheat the oven to 190°C/375°F/Gas Mark 5. Line a 12-hole bun tray with paper cases.

2 Place all the cupcake ingredients in a large bowl and beat with an electric mixer for about 2 minutes until smooth. Fill the paper cases halfway up with the mixture. Bake for about 15 minutes until firm, risen and golden. Remove to a wire rack to cool.

3 To decorate the cupcakes, first line an egg box with foil and set aside. Colour the sugarpaste icing with pink paste food colouring. Make a small cone shape, then roll a pea-size piece of sugarpaste into a ball. Flatten out the ball into a petal shape and wrap this round the cone shape. Continue adding more petals to make a rose, then trim the thick base, place in the egg box and leave to dry out for 2 hours.

4 Blend the fondant icing sugar with a little water to make a thick icing of spreading consistency, then colour this pale pink. Smooth over the top of each cupcake and decorate with the roses immediately. Leave to set for 1 hour. Keep for 1 day in an airtight container.

Ingredients SERVES 12

125 g/4 oz caster sugar
125 g/4 oz soft tub margarine
2 medium eggs
125 g/4 oz self-raising flour
1 tsp baking powder
1 tsp rosewater

To decorate:
50 g/2 oz ready-to-roll
 sugarpaste icing
pink paste food colouring
350 g/12 oz fondant
 icing sugar

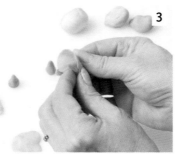

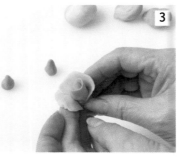

White Chocolate & Passion Fruit Cake

1 Preheat the oven to 180°C/350°F/Gas Mark 4, 10 minutes before baking. Lightly oil and line two 20.5 cm/8 inch cake tins. Melt the white chocolate, stir in 125 ml/4 fl oz warm water and stir, then leave to cool. Whisk the butter and sugar together until light and fluffy, then add the eggs, one at a time, beating well after each addition. Beat in the chocolate mixture, sour cream and sifted flours. Divide the mixture into eight portions. Spread one portion into each of the tins. Bake in the oven for 10 minutes, or until firm, then turn out onto wire racks. Repeat with the remaining mixture to make eight cake layers.

2 For the icing, place 125 ml/4 fl oz water with 50 g/2 oz of the sugar in a saucepan. Heat gently, stirring, until the sugar has dissolved. Bring to the boil and simmer for 2 minutes. Remove from the heat, cool, then add 2 tablespoons of the passion fruit juice. Reserve. Blend the remaining sugar with 50 ml/2 fl oz water in a saucepan and stir constantly over a low heat, without boiling, until the sugar has dissolved. Remove from the heat and cool. Stir in the remaining juice and the seeds. Cool, then strain. Using an electric whisk, beat the butter in a bowl until very pale. Gradually beat in the syrup.

3 Place one layer of cake on a serving plate. Brush with the syrup and spread with a thin layer of icing. Repeat with the remaining cake, syrup and icing. Cover the cake with the remaining icing. Press the grated chocolate into the top and sides to decorate.

Ingredients   SERVES 8–10

125 g/4 oz white chocolate
125 g/4 oz butter
225 g/8 oz caster sugar
2 medium eggs
125 ml/4 fl oz sour cream
200 g/7 oz plain flour, sifted
75 g/3 oz self-raising flour, sifted
125 g/4 oz white chocolate, coarsely grated, to decorate

For the icing:

200 g/7 oz caster sugar
4 tbsp passion fruit juice (about 8–10 passion fruit, sieved)
1 1/2 tbsp passion fruit seeds
250 g/9 oz unsalted butter

Food Fact

Passion fruit is available from large supermarkets. It adds a sweet/sour flavour that goes particularly well with white chocolate.

Indulgent Chocolate Squares

1 Preheat the oven to 180°C/350°F/Gas Mark 4, 10 minutes before baking. Oil and line a deep 20.5 cm/8 inch square cake tin with nonstick baking parchment. Melt 225 g/8 oz of the dark chocolate in a heatproof bowl set over a saucepan of almost boiling water. Stir until smooth, then leave until just cool, but not beginning to set.

2 Beat the butter and sugar until light and fluffy. Stir in the melted chocolate, ground almonds, egg yolks, cocoa powder and breadcrumbs. Whisk the egg whites until stiff peaks form, then stir a large spoonful into the chocolate mixture. Gently fold in the rest, then pour the mixture into the prepared tin.

3 Bake on the centre shelf in the preheated oven for 1¼ hours, or until firm, covering the top with foil after 45 minutes to prevent it over–browning. Leave in the tin for 20 minutes, then turn out onto a wire rack and leave to cool.

4 Melt the remaining 125 g/4 oz plain chocolate with the cream in a heatproof bowl set over a saucepan of almost boiling water, stirring occasionally. Leave to cool for 20 minutes, or until thickened slightly.

5 Spread the topping over the cake. Scatter over the white and milk chocolate and leave to set. Cut into 16 squares and serve decorated with a few freshly sliced strawberries, then serve.

Ingredients   SERVE 16

350 g/12 oz dark chocolate
175 g/6 oz butter, softened
175 g/6 oz soft light brown suga
175 g/6 oz ground almonds
6 large eggs, separated
3 tbsp cocoa powder, sifted
75 g/3 oz fresh brown breadcrumbs
125 ml/4 fl oz double cream
50 g/2 oz white chocolate, chopped
50 g/2 oz milk chocolate, choppe
few freshly sliced strawberries,
  to decorate

Helpful Hint

To prevent the foil from coming off the top of the tin, especially in a fan assisted oven, fold the foil around the edge, rather than simply laying it on top.

Birthday Numbers Cupcakes

1 Preheat the oven to 180°C/350°F/Gas Mark 4. Line one or two 12-hole bun trays with 12–14 paper fairy-cake cases or silicone moulds, depending on the depth of the holes.

2 Sift the flour into a bowl and stir together with the caster sugar. Add the margarine, eggs and vanilla extract and beat together for about 2 minutes until smooth.

3 Spoon into the cases and bake for 15–20 minutes until golden and firm to the touch. Turn out on a wire rack. When cool, trim the tops flat if they have peaked slightly.

4 To decorate, colour batches of sugarpaste in bright colours. Dust a clean surface lightly with icing sugar. Thinly roll each colour of sugarpaste and cut out numbers using a set of cutters. Leave these for 2 hours to dry and harden.

5 Using a palette knife, spread the buttercream thickly onto the top of each cupcake. Place a small candle into each cupcake and stand the number up against this. Serve within 8 hours as the numbers may start to soften.

Ingredients   MAKES 12–14

125 g/4 oz self-raising flour
125 g/4 oz caster sugar
125 g/4 oz soft margarine
2 medium eggs, beaten
1 tsp vanilla extract

To decorate:
225 g/8 oz ready-to-roll sugarpaste
paste food colourings
icing sugar, for dusting
1 batch buttercream (*see* page 14)
small candles

Whole Orange & Chocolate Cake with Marmalade Cream

1   Preheat the oven to 180°C/350°F/Gas Mark 4, 10 minutes before baking. Lightly oil and line the base of a 900 g/2 lb loaf tin. Place the orange in a small saucepan, cover with cold water and bring to the boil. Simmer for 1 hour until completely soft. Drain and leave to cool. Place 2 egg yolks, 1 whole egg and the sugar in a heatproof bowl set over a saucepan of simmering water and whisk until doubled in bulk. Remove from the heat and continue to whisk for 5 minutes until cooled.

2   Cut the whole orange in half and discard the seeds, then place into a food processor or blender and blend to a purée. Carefully fold the purée into the egg yolk mixture with the ground almonds and melted chocolate. Whisk the egg whites until stiff peaks form. Fold a large spoonful of the egg whites into the chocolate mixture, then gently fold the remaining egg whites into the mixture.

3   Pour into the tin and bake in the oven for 50 minutes, or until firm and a skewer inserted into the centre comes out clean. Cool in the tin before turning out and carefully discarding the lining paper. Meanwhile, whip the double cream until just thickened. In another bowl, blend the soft cheese with the icing sugar and marmalade until smooth, then fold in the double cream. Chill the marmalade cream in the refrigerator until required. Decorate with orange zest and serve the cake cut into slices with the marmalade cream.

Ingredients

SERVES 5–8

1 small orange, scrubbed
2 medium eggs, separated,
   plus 1 whole egg
150 g/5 oz caster sugar
125 g/4 oz ground almonds
75 g/3 oz dark chocolate, melted
100 ml/3^1/$_2$ fl oz double cream
200 g/7 oz full-fat soft cheese
25 g/1 oz icing sugar
2 tbsp orange marmalade
orange zest, to decorate

Tasty Tip
This cake contains no flour and is therefore likely to sink in the centre on cooling. This is normal and does not mean that the cake is not cooked.

Peach & White Chocolate Gateau

1 Preheat the oven to 170°C/325°F/Gas Mark 3, 10 minutes before baking. Lightly oil and line a deep 23 cm/9 inch round cake tin. Cream the butter, orange zest and sugar together until light and fluffy. Add the eggs, one at a time, beating well after each addition, then beat in the cooled white chocolate.

2 Add the flour and 175 ml/6 fl oz water in two batches. Spoon into the prepared tin and bake in the preheated oven for 1¹/₂ hours, or until firm. Leave to stand for at least 5 minutes before turning out onto a wire rack to cool completely.

3 To make the filling, place the peaches in a bowl and pour over the liqueur. Leave to stand for 30 minutes. Whip the cream with the icing sugar until soft peaks form, then fold in the peach mixture.

4 Split the cold cake in to three layers, place one layer on a serving plate and spread with half the peach filling. Top with a second sponge layer and spread with the remaining peach filling. Top with the remaining cake.

5 Whip the cream and icing sugar together until soft peaks form. Spread over the top and sides of the cake, piping some onto the top, if liked. Press the hazelnuts into the side of the cake and, if liked, sprinkle a few on top. Chill in the refrigerator until required. Serve cut into slices. Store the cake in the refrigerator.

Ingredients   SERVES 8–10

175 g/6 oz unsalted butter, softened
2 tsp grated orange zest
175 g/6 oz caster sugar
3 medium eggs
100 g/3¹/₂ oz white chocolate, melted and cooled
225 g/8 oz self-raising flour, sifted
300 ml/¹/₂ pint double cream
40 g/1¹/₂ oz icing sugar
125 g/4 oz hazelnuts, toasted and chopped

For the peach filling:
2 ripe peaches, peeled and chopped
2 tbsp peach or orange liqueur
300 ml/¹/₂ pint double cream
40 g/1¹/₂ oz icing sugar

Tasty Tip
When fresh peaches are out of season, use drained and chopped canned peaches instead.

Sachertorte

1 Preheat the oven to 180°C/350°F/Gas Mark 4, 10 minutes before baking. Lightly oil and line a deep 23 cm/9 inch cake tin. Melt the 150 g/5 oz of chocolate in a heatproof bowl set over a saucepan of simmering water. Stir in 1 tablespoon water; leave to cool.

2 Beat the butter and 125 g/4 oz of the sugar together until light and fluffy. Beat in the egg yolks, one at a time, beating well after each addition. Stir in the melted chocolate, then the flour. In a clean grease-free bowl, whisk the egg whites until stiff peaks form, then whisk in the remaining sugar. Fold into the chocolate mixture and spoon into the tin. Bake in the oven for 30 minutes until firm. Leave for 5 minutes, then turn out onto a wire rack to cool. Leave the cake upside down.

3 To decorate, split the cake in two and place one half on a plate. Heat the jam and rub through a fine sieve. Brush half the jam onto the first cake half, then cover with the remaining half and brush with the remaining jam. Leave at room temperature for 1 hour, or until the jam has set. Place the dark chocolate with the butter into a heatproof bowl set over a saucepan of simmering water and heat until the chocolate has melted. Stir occasionally until smooth, then leave until thickened. Use to cover the cake. Melt the milk-chocolate in a heatproof bowl set over a saucepan of simmering water. Place in a small greaseproof piping bag and snip a small hole at the tip. Pipe 'Sacher' with a large 'S' on the top. Leave to set at room temperature.

Ingredients   SERVES 10–12

150 g/5 oz dark chocolate
150 g/5 oz unsalted butter, softened
125 g/4 oz caster sugar, plus 2 tbsp
3 medium eggs, separated
150 g/5 oz plain flour, sifted

To decorate:
225 g/8 oz apricot jam
125 g/4 oz dark chocolate, chopped
125 g/4 oz unsalted butter
25 g/1 oz milk chocolate

Food Fact
In 1832, the Viennese foreign minister asked a Vienna hotel to prepare an especially tempting cake. The head pastry chef was ill and so the task fell to second year apprentice, Franz Sacher, who presented this delightful cake.

2

2

3

Valentine Heart Cupcakes

1 Preheat the oven to 180°C/350°F/Gas Mark 4 and line a 12–hole muffin tray with deep paper cases.

2 Place the butter, sugar, eggs, vanilla extract and milk in a bowl, then sift in the flour and baking powder. Beat together for about 2 minutes with an electric hand mixer until pale and fluffy. Spoon into the paper cases and bake for 20–25 minutes until firm and golden. Cool on a wire rack.

3 To decorate, colour one third of the sugarpaste pink and one third red, leaving the rest white. Dust a clean flat surface with icing sugar. Roll out the sugarpaste thinly and, using a cutter, cut out pink, red and white heart shapes, then leave to dry flat and harden on a board covered with clingfilm for 2 hours.

4 Colour the cream cheese frosting pale pink and place in a piping bag fitted with a star nozzle. Pipe a swirl on top of each cupcake and decorate with the hearts. Keep in a cool place for up to 2 days.

Ingredients   MAKES 12

150 g/5 oz butter, softened
150 g/5 oz caster sugar
3 medium eggs, beaten
1 tsp vanilla extract
2 tbsp milk
150 g/5 oz self–raising flour
$^1/_2$ tsp baking powder

To decorate:

pink and red paste food colouring
225 g/8 oz ready–to–roll sugarpaste
icing sugar, for dusting
1 batch cream cheese frosting (*see* page 14)

Black Forest Gateau

1 Preheat the oven to 150°C/300°F/Gas Mark 2, 5 minutes before baking. Lightly oil and line a deep 23 cm/9 inch cake tin. Melt the butter in a large saucepan. Blend the coffee with the hot water, add to the butter with the chocolate and sugar and heat gently, stirring until smooth. Pour into a bowl and leave until just warm. Sift together the flours and cocoa powder. Using an electric mixer, whisk the chocolate mixture on a low speed, then gradually whisk in the dry ingredients. Whisk in the eggs one at a time, then the vanilla extract. Pour the mixture into the tin and bake in the oven for 1 ³/₄ hours, or until firm and a skewer inserted into the centre comes out clean. Leave in the tin for 5 minutes to cool slightly before turning out onto a wire rack.

2 Place the cherries and their juice in a small saucepan and heat gently. Blend the arrowroot with 2 teaspoons water until smooth, then stir into the cherries. Cook, stirring, until the liquid thickens. Simmer very gently for 2 minutes, then leave until cold.

3 Whisk the double cream until thick. Trim the top of the cake if necessary, then split the cake into three layers. Brush the base of the cake with half the kirsch. Top with a layer of cream and one third of the cherries. Repeat the layering, then place the third layer on top. Reserve a little cream for decorating and use the remainder to cover the top and sides of the cake. Pipe a decorative edge around the cake, then arrange the remaining cherries in the centre and serve.

Ingredients   CUTS INTO
10–12 SLICES

250 g/9 oz butter
1 tbsp instant coffee granules
350 ml/12 fl oz hot water
200 g/7 oz dark chocolate, chopped
    or broken
400 g/14 oz caster sugar
225 g/8 oz self–raising flour
150 g/5 oz plain flour
50 g/2 oz cocoa powder
2 medium eggs
2 tsp vanilla extract
2 x 400 g cans stoned cherries in juice
2 tsp arrowroot
600 ml/1 pint double cream
50 ml/2 fl oz kirsch

Helpful Hint
The cake can be assembled and served straightaway but will benefit from being refrigerated for 1–2 hours so that the cream sets slightly. This will make slicing easier.

Grated Chocolate Roulade

1 Preheat the oven to 180°C/350°F/Gas Mark 4, 10 minutes before baking. Lightly oil and line a 20.5 cm x 30.5 cm/8 inch x 12 inch Swiss roll tin. Beat the egg yolks and sugar with an electric mixer for 5 minutes, or until thick, then stir in 2 tablespoons hot water and the grated chocolate. Finally, fold in the sifted flour.

2 Whisk the egg whites until stiff, then fold 1–2 tablespoons of egg white into the chocolate mixture. Mix lightly, then gently fold in the remaining egg white. Pour into the prepared tin and bake in the preheated oven for about 12 minutes or until firm.

3 Place a large sheet of nonstick baking parchment onto a work surface and sprinkle liberally with caster sugar. Turn the cake onto the baking parchment, discard the lining paper and trim away the crisp edges. Roll up as for a Swiss roll cake, leave for 2 minutes, then unroll and leave to cool.

4 Beat the double cream with the icing sugar and vanilla extract until thick. Reserve a little for decoration, then spread the remaining cream over the cake, leaving a 2.5 cm/1 inch border all round. Using the greaseproof paper, roll up from a short end.

5 Carefully transfer the roulade to a large serving plate and use the reserved cream to decorate the top. Add the chocolate curls just before serving, then cut into slices and serve. Store in the refrigerator.

Ingredients

CUTS INTO
8 SLICES

4 medium eggs, separated
125 g/4 oz caster sugar
65 g/2$^1/_2$ oz dark chocolate, grated
75 g/3 oz self-raising flour, sifted
2 tbsp caster sugar, plus extra for
  sprinkling
150 ml/$^1/_4$ pint double cream
2 tsp icing sugar
1 tsp vanilla extract
chocolate curls, to decorate

Helpful Hint

Make sure to leave a border around the cream before rolling up the roulade or all the cream will squeeze out of the ends.

1

3

4

White Chocolate & Raspberry Mousse Gateau

1 Preheat the oven to 190°C/375°F/Gas Mark 5, 10 minutes before baking. Oil and line two 23 cm/9 inch cake tins. Whisk the eggs and sugar until thick and creamy and the whisk leaves a trail in the mixture. Fold in the flour and cornflour, then divide between the tins. Bake in the oven for 12–15 minutes until risen and firm. Cool in the tins, then turn out onto wire racks.

2 Place the gelatine with 4 tablespoons cold water in a dish and leave to soften for 5 minutes. Purée half the raspberries, press through a sieve, then heat until nearly boiling. Squeeze out excess water from the gelatine, add to the purée and stir until dissolved. Reserve. Melt 175 g/6 oz of the chocolate in a bowl set over a saucepan of simmering water. Leave to cool, then stir in the fromage frais and purée. Whisk the egg whites until stiff and whisk in the sugar. Fold into the raspberry mixture with the raspberries. Line the sides of a 23 cm/9 inch springform tin with baking parchment. Place 1 layer of cake in the base and sprinkle with half the liqueur. Pour in the raspberry mixture and top with the second cake. Brush with the remaining liqueur. Press down and chill for 4 hours. Unmould onto a plate. Cut a strip of double thickness baking parchment to fit around and 1 cm/½ inch higher than the cake. Melt the remaining chocolate and spread thickly onto the parchment. Leave until just setting. Wrap around the cake and freeze for 15 minutes. Peel away the parchment. Whip the cream until thick and spread over the top. Decorate with raspberries.

Ingredients
CUTS INTO 8 SLICES

4 medium eggs
125 g/4 oz caster sugar
75 g/3 oz plain flour, sifted
25 g/1 oz cornflour, sifted
3 gelatine leaves
450 g/1 lb raspberries, thawed if frozen
400 g/14 oz white chocolate
200 g/7 oz plain fromage frais
2 medium egg whites
25 g/1 oz caster sugar
4 tbsp raspberry or orange liqueur
200 ml/7 fl oz double cream
fresh raspberries, halved, to decorate

Helpful Hint
Do not try to wrap the chocolate-covered parchment around the cake before it is nearly set or it will run down and be uneven.

Coffee & Walnut Gateau with Brandied Prunes

1 Preheat the oven to 180°C/350°F/Gas Mark 4, 10 minutes before baking. Soak the prunes with the tea and brandy for 3–4 hours, or overnight. Oil and line the bases of two 23 cm/ 9 inch tins. Chop three quarters of the walnuts in a food processor. Add the flour, baking powder and coffee and blend until finely ground.

2 Whisk the egg whites with the cream of tartar until soft peaks form. Sprinkle in one third of the sugar, 2 tablespoons at a time, until stiff peaks form. In another bowl, beat the egg yolks, oil and the remaining sugar until thick. Alternately fold in the nut mixture and egg whites until just blended. Divide the mixture evenly between the tins, smoothing the tops. Bake in the oven for 30–35 minutes until the tops of the cakes spring back when lightly pressed with a clean finger. Remove from the oven and cool. Remove from the tins and discard the lining paper.

3 Drain the prunes, reserving the liquid. Dry on kitchen paper, then chop and reserve. Whisk the cream with the icing sugar and liqueur until soft peaks form. Spoon one eighth of the cream into a pastry bag fitted with a star nozzle. Cut the cake layers in half horizontally. Sprinkle each cut side with 1 tablespoon of the reserved prune-soaking liquid. Sandwich the cakes together with half of the cream and all of the prunes. Spread the remaining cream around the sides and press in the reserved chopped walnuts. Pipe rosettes around the edge, decorate with walnut halves and serve.

Ingredients
CUTS INTO 10–12 SLICES

For the prunes:
225 g/8 oz ready-to-eat pitted dried prunes
150 ml/$^1/_4$ pint cold tea
3 tbsp brandy

For the cake:
450 g/1 lb walnut pieces
50 g/2 oz self-raising flour
$^1/_2$ tsp baking powder
1 tsp instant coffee powder (not granules)
5 large eggs, separated
$^1/_4$ tsp cream of tartar
150 g/5 oz caster sugar
2 tbsp sunflower oil
8 walnut halves, to decorate

For the filling:
600 ml/1 pint double cream
4 tbsp icing sugar, sifted
2 tbsp coffee-flavoured liqueur

1

3

3

Black & White Torte

1 Preheat the oven to 180°C/350°F/Gas Mark 4, 10 minutes before baking. Lightly oil and line a 23 cm/9 inch round cake tin. Beat the eggs and sugar in a large bowl until thick and creamy. Sift together the cornflour, plain flour and self-raising flour three times, then lightly fold into the egg mixture. Spoon the mixture into the tin and bake in the oven for 35–40 minutes until firm. Turn the cake out onto a wire rack and leave to cool.

2 Place 300 ml/$^1/_2$ pint of the double cream in a saucepan and bring to the boil. Remove from the heat and add the dark chocolate and 1 tablespoon of the liqueur. Stir until smooth. Repeat using the remaining cream, white chocolate and 2 tablespoons of the liqueur. Refrigerate for 2 hours, then whisk each mixture until thick and creamy.

3 Place the dark chocolate mixture in a piping bag fitted with a plain nozzle and place half the white chocolate mixture in a separate piping bag fitted with a plain nozzle. Reserve the remaining white chocolate mixture.

4 Split the cold cake horizontally into two layers. Brush or drizzle the remaining 3 tablespoons of liqueur over the cakes. Put one layer onto a plate. Pipe alternating rings of white and dark chocolate mixture to cover the first layer of cake. Use the reserved white chocolate mixture to cover the top and sides of the cake. Dust with cocoa powder, cut into slices and serve.

Ingredients   SERVES 8–10

4 medium eggs
150 g/5 oz caster sugar
50 g/2 oz cornflour
50 g/2 oz plain flour
50 g/2 oz self-raising flour
900 ml/1$^1/_2$ pints double cream
150 g/5 oz dark chocolate, choppe
6 tbsp Grand Marnier, or other
 orange liqueur
300 g/11 oz white chocolate,
 chopped
cocoa powder, for dusting

Father's Day Cupcakes

1 Preheat the oven to 180°C/350°F/Gas Mark 4. Line two 12-hole bun trays with 14 paper fairy-cake cases or silicone moulds.

2 Sift the flour into a bowl and stir together with the caster sugar. Add the margarine, eggs and vanilla extract and beat together for about 2 minutes until smooth.

3 Spoon into the cases and bake for 15–20 minutes until golden and firm to the touch. Turn out on a wire rack. When cool, trim the tops flat if they have peaked slightly.

4 To decorate, colour half the buttercream yellow and the other half orange and swirl over the top of each cupcake. Dust a clean flat surface with icing sugar. Colour the sugarpaste light blue and roll out thinly. Stamp out large stars 4 cm/1½ inches wide and place these on the buttercream.

5 Make up the royal icing mix (see page 14) and place in a paper piping bag with the end snipped away and pipe 'Dad' or names on the stars. Decorate with the edible silver balls. Keep for 3 days in an airtight container.

Ingredients   MAKES 14

125 g/4 oz self-raising flour
125 g/4 oz caster sugar
125 g/4 oz soft margarine
2 medium eggs, beaten
1 tsp vanilla extract

To decorate:
1 batch buttercream (see page 14)
yellow, orange and blue paste food colouring
225 g/8 oz ready-to-roll sugarpaste
50 g/2 oz royal icing sugar
edible silver balls

Cranberry & White Chocolate Cake

1 Preheat the oven to 180°C/350°F/Gas Mark 4, 10 minutes before baking. Lightly oil and flour a 23 cm/9 inch kugelhopf tin or ring tin. Using an electric mixer, cream the butter and cheese with the sugars until light and fluffy. Add the grated orange zest and vanilla extract and beat until smooth, then beat in the eggs, 1 at a time.

2 Sift the flour and baking powder together and stir into the creamed mixture, beating well after each addition. Fold in the cranberries and 175 g/6 oz of the white chocolate. Spoon into the prepared tin and bake in the preheated oven for 1 hour, or until firm and a skewer inserted into the centre comes out clean. Cool in the tin before turning out onto on a wire rack.

3 Melt the remaining white chocolate, stir until smooth, then stir in the orange juice and leave to cool until thickened. Transfer the cake to a serving plate and spoon over the white chocolate and orange glaze. Leave to set.

Ingredients   SERVES 4

225 g/8 oz butter, softened
250 g/9 oz full-fat soft cheese
150 g/5 oz soft light brown sugar
200 g/7 oz caster sugar
grated zest of $1/_2$ orange
1 tsp vanilla extract
4 medium eggs
375 g/13 oz plain flour
2 tsp baking powder
200 g/7 oz cranberries, thawed
    if frozen
225 g/8 oz white chocolate,
    roughly chopped
2 tbsp orange juice

Tasty Tip

If fresh or frozen cranberries are not available, substitute with peeled and diced Bramley cooking apple, raisins, dried cranberries or ready-to-eat chopped dried apricots.

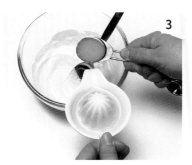

Celebration Fruit Cake

1 Preheat the oven to 170°C/325°F/Gas Mark 3, 10 minutes before baking. Heat the butter and sugar in a saucepan until the sugar has dissolved, stirring frequently. Add the pineapple and juice, dried fruits and peel. Bring to the boil, simmer for 3 minutes, stirring occasionally, then remove from the heat to cool completely.

2 Lightly oil and line the base of a 20.5 x 7.5 cm/8 x 3 inch loose-bottomed cake tin with nonstick baking parchment. Sift the flour, bicarbonate of soda, spices and salt into a bowl.

3 Add the boiled fruit mixture to the flour with the eggs and mix. Spoon into the tin and smooth the top. Bake in the preheated oven for 1¼ hours, or until a skewer inserted into the centre comes out clean. (If the cake is browning too quickly, cover loosely with foil and reduce the oven temperature.)

4 Remove and cool completely before removing from the tin and discarding the lining paper. Arrange the nuts, cherries and prunes or dates in an attractive pattern on top of the cake. Heat the honey and brush over the topping to glaze.

5 Alternatively, toss the nuts and fruits in the warm honey and spread evenly over the top of the cake. Cool completely and store in a cake tin for a day or two before serving, to allow the flavours to develop.

Ingredients
CUTS INTO
12 SLICES

125 g/4 oz butter or margarine
125 g/4 oz soft dark brown sugar
380 g can crushed pineapple
150 g/5 oz raisins
150 g/5 oz sultanas
125 g/4 oz crystallised ginger, chopped
125 g/4 oz glacé cherries, chopped
125 g/4 oz mixed cut peel
225 g/8 oz self-raising flour
1 tsp bicarbonate of soda
2 tsp mixed spice
1 tsp ground cinnamon
½ tsp salt
2 large eggs, beaten

For the topping:
100 g/3½ oz pecan or walnut halves, lightly toasted
125 g/4 oz varied glacé cherries
100 g/3½ oz pitted prunes or dates
2 tbsp clear honey, to decorate

1

3

4

Simnel Easter Muffins

1 Preheat the oven to 190°C/375°F/Gas Mark 5. Line a deep muffin tray with six to eight paper cases, depending on the depth of the holes. Weigh 25 g/1 oz of the marzipan and roll into long thin strips. Grate or chop the remaining marzipan into small chunks.

2 Whisk the milk, sugar and eggs together in a jug. Sift the flour and spice into a bowl, then stir together with the fruit, cherries and the marzipan chunks. Pour the milk mixture into the flour mixture along with the melted butter. Mix until combined.

3 Spoon into the paper cases and make a cross over the top of each using two marzipan strips. Bake for about 20 minutes until firm in the centre. Cool in the tins for 3 minutes, then turn out to cool on a wire rack. Eat warm or cold. Keep for 24 hours sealed in an airtight container.

Ingredients MAKES 6–8

125 g/4 oz yellow marzipan
150 ml/¹/₄ pint milk
50 g/2 oz soft light brown sugar
2 medium eggs
175 g/6 oz self-raising flour
¹/₂ tsp mixed spice
75 g/3 oz mixed dried fruit
50 g/2 oz glacé cherries, washed
   and chopped
75 g/3 oz butter, melted
   and cooled

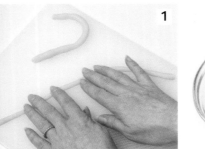

Chocolate Buttermilk Cake

1 Preheat the oven to 180°C/350°F/Gas Mark 4, 10 minutes before baking. Lightly oil and line a deep 23 cm/9 inch round cake tin. Cream together the butter, vanilla extract and sugar until light and fluffy, then beat in the egg yolks, one at a time.

2 Sift together the flour and cocoa powder and fold into the egg mixture together with the buttermilk. Whisk the egg whites until soft peaks form and fold carefully into the chocolate mixture in two batches. Spoon the mixture into the prepared tin and bake in the preheated oven for 1 hour, or until firm. Cool slightly, then turn out onto a wire rack and leave until completely cold.

3 Place the chocolate and butter together in a heatproof bowl set over a saucepan of simmering water and heat until melted. Stir until smooth, then leave at room temperature until the chocolate is thick enough to spread.

4 Split the cake horizontally in half. Use some of the chocolate mixture to sandwich the two halves together. Spread and decorate the top of the cake with the remaining chocolate mixture. Finally, whip the cream until soft peaks form and use to spread around the sides of the cake. Chill in the refrigerator until required. Serve cut into slices. Store in the refrigerator.

Ingredients

CUTS INTO 8–10 SLICES

175 g/6 oz butter
1 tsp vanilla extract
350 g/12 oz caster sugar
4 medium eggs, separated
100 g/3$\frac{1}{2}$ oz self-raising flour
40 g/1$\frac{1}{2}$ oz cocoa powder
175 ml/6 fl oz buttermilk
200 g/7 oz dark chocolate
100 g/3$\frac{1}{2}$ oz butter
300 ml/$\frac{1}{2}$ pint double cream

Tasty Tip

If buttermilk is unavailable, measure 175 ml/6 fl oz full-fat milk and add 2 teaspoons lemon juice or white wine vinegar. Leave to stand for 1 hour at room temperature and then use as above.

Winter Wedding Cupcakes

1 Preheat the oven to 180°C/350°F/Gas Mark 4. Line one or two 12-hole muffin trays with 12–14 deep paper cases, depending on the depth of the holes.

2 Beat the butter and sugar together until light and fluffy, then beat in the eggs a little at a time, adding 1 tsp flour with each addition. Sift in the remaining flour and the spice, add the orange zest and juice, treacle and dried fruit to the bowl and fold together until the mixture is blended. Spoon into the tins and bake for 30 minutes until firm in the centre and a skewer comes out clean. Leave to cool in the tins for 15 minutes, then turn out onto a wire rack. Store undecorated in an airtight container for up to 3 weeks, or freeze until needed.

3 To decorate the cupcakes, trim the top of each cake level, then brush with apricot glaze. Roll out the almond paste and cut out eight discs 6 cm/2¹/₂ inches wide. Place these over the glaze and press level. Leave to dry for 24 hours if possible.

4 Dust a clean flat surface with icing sugar. Roll out the sugarpaste and stamp out holly leaf and ivy shapes. Leave to dry for 2 hours on nonstick baking parchment or clingfilm. Swirl the royal icing over the top of each cupcake. Press in the holly and ivy shapes and leave to set for 2 hours. Once decorated, keep in an airtight container for 3 days.

Ingredients   MAKES 12–14

125 g/4 oz butter, softened
125 g/4 oz soft dark
    muscovado sugar
2 medium eggs, beaten
225 g/8 oz self-raising flour
1 tsp ground mixed spice
finely grated zest and 1 tbsp juice
    from 1 orange
1 tbsp black treacle
350 g/12 oz mixed dried fruit

To decorate:

3 tbsp sieved apricot glaze (see
    page 15)
450 g/1 lb almond paste (see
    page 15)
icing sugar, for dusting
225 g/8 oz ready-to-roll sugarpaste
225 g/8 oz royal icing
fancy paper wrappers (optional)

2

2

4

Raspberry & Hazelnut Meringue Cake

1 Preheat the oven to 140°C/275°F/Gas Mark 1. Line two baking sheets with nonstick baking parchment and draw a 20.5 cm/8 inch circle on each. Whisk the egg whites and cream of tartar until soft peaks form, then gradually beat in the sugar, 2 tablespoons at a time.

2 Beat well after each addition until the whites are stiff and glossy. Using a metal spoon or rubber spatula, gently fold in the ground hazelnuts.

3 Divide the mixture evenly between the two circles and spread neatly. Swirl one of the circles to make a decorative top layer. Bake in the preheated oven for about 1½ hours until crisp and dry. Turn off the oven and allow the meringues to cool for 1 hour. Transfer to a wire rack to cool completely. Carefully peel off the papers.

4 For the filling, whip the cream, icing sugar and liqueur, if using, together until soft peaks form. Place the flat round on a serving plate. Spread over most of the cream, reserving some for decorating and arrange the raspberries in concentric circles over the cream.

5 Place the swirly meringue on top of the cream and raspberries, pressing down gently. Pipe the remaining cream onto the meringue and decorate with a few raspberries and serve.

Ingredients

CUTS INTO
8 SLICES

For the meringue:
4 large egg whites
¼ tsp cream of tartar
225 g/8 oz caster sugar
75 g/3 oz hazelnuts, skinned, toasted and finely ground

For the filling:
300 ml/½ pint double cream
1 tbsp icing sugar
1–2 tbsp raspberry–flavoured liqueur (optional)
350 g/12 oz fresh raspberries

Helpful Hint
It is essential when whisking egg whites that the bowl being used is completely clean and dry, as any grease or oil will prevent the egg whites from gaining the volume needed.

Chocolate Mousse Cake

1 Preheat the oven to 180°C/350°F/Gas Mark 4, 10 minutes before baking. Lightly oil and line the bases of two 20.5 cm/8 inch springform tins with baking parchment. Melt the chocolate and butter in a bowl set over a saucepan of simmering water. Stir until smooth. Remove from the heat and stir in the brandy.

2 Whisk the egg yolks and all but 2 tablespoons of the sugar until thick and creamy. Slowly beat in the chocolate mixture until smooth and well blended. Whisk the egg whites until soft peaks form, then sprinkle over the remaining sugar and whisk until stiff but not dry. Fold a large spoonful of the whites into the chocolate. Gently fold in the rest. Divide about two thirds of the mixture evenly between the tins, tapping to distribute it evenly. Bake in the oven for about 20 minutes until the cakes are well risen and set. Cool for at least 1 hour. Loosen the edges of the cake layers with a knife. Using the fingertips, lightly press the crusty edges down. Pour the rest of the mousse over one layer, spreading until even. Carefully unclip the side, remove the other cake from the tin and gently invert onto the mousse, bottom side up. Discard the paper and chill for 4–6 hours until set.

3 To make the glaze, melt the cream and chocolate with the brandy in a heavy saucepan and stir until smooth. Cool until thickened. Unclip the side of the tin and place the cake on a wire rack. Cover the cake with half the glaze. Allow to set, then decorate with chocolate curls. Serve with heated glaze and dotted with cream.

Ingredients   SERVES 8–10

For the cake:
450 g/1 lb dark chocolate, chopped
125 g/4 oz butter, softened
3 tbsp brandy
9 large eggs, separated
150 g/5 oz caster sugar

For the chocolate glaze:
225 ml/8 fl oz double cream
225 g/8 oz dark chocolate, chopped
2 tbsp brandy
1 tbsp single cream and white
    chocolate curls, to decorate

Food Fact
Wonderfully rich and delicious served with a fruity compote – why not try making cherry compote using either fresh if in season or otherwise tinned in fruit juice. Stone the cherries, or drain and then simmer on a low heat with a little apple juice until reduced.

Marzipan Cake

1 Grind the blanched almonds in a food processor until fairly fine. Mix with 200 g/7 oz of the icing sugar. Beat the egg whites until stiff then fold into the almond mixture using a metal spoon or rubber spatula to form a stiffish dough. It will still be quite sticky but will firm up as it rests. Leave for 30 minutes.

2 Dust a work surface very generously with some of the remaining icing sugar so that the marzipan does not stick. Roll out two thirds of the marzipan onto a large sheet to a thickness of about 5 mm/$^1/_4$ inch. Use to line a sloping–sided baking dish with a base measuring 25.5 cm x 20.5 cm/10 x 8 inches. Trim the edges and put any trimmings with the remainder of the marzipan.

3 Cut the Madeira cake into thin slices and make a layer of sponge to cover the bottom of the marzipan. Sprinkle with the Marsala wine. Beat the ricotta with the sugar and add the lemon zest, candied peel and cherries. Spread this over the sponge. Slice the peaches and put them on top of the ricotta. Whip the cream and spread it over the peaches. Roll out the remaining marzipan and lay it over the cream to seal the whole cake, pressing down gently to remove any air. Press the edges of the marzipan together. Chill in the refrigerator for 2 hours.

4 Turn the cake out onto a serving plate and dust generously with icing sugar. Slice thickly and serve immediately.

Ingredients   SERVES 1?–14

450 g/1 lb blanched almonds
300 g/11 oz icing sugar (include?
    sugar for dusting and rolling)
4 medium egg whites
125 g/4 oz Madeira cake
2 tbsp Marsala wine
225 g/8 oz ricotta cheese
50 g/2 oz caster sugar
grated zest of 1 lemon
50 g/2 oz candied peel,
    finely chopped
25 g/1 oz glacé cherries,
    finely chopped
425 g can peach halves, drained
200 ml/$^1/_3$ pint double cream

Helpful Hint

Homemade marzipan is stickier tha?
commercially prepared versions. Us?
plenty of icing sugar when rolling it?s
well as sprinkling the dish liberally
with it.

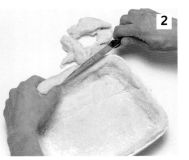

Chocolate Box Cake

1 Preheat the oven to 180°C/350°F/Gas Mark 4, 10 minutes before baking. Lightly oil and flour a 20.5 cm/8 inch square cake tin. Sift the flour and baking powder into a large bowl and stir in the sugar. Using an electric whisk, beat in the butter and eggs. Blend the cocoa powder with 1 tablespoon water, then beat into the creamed mixture. Turn into the tin and bake in the oven for about 25 minutes, or until well risen and cooked. Remove and cool before removing the cake from the tin.

2 For the chocolate box, break the chocolate into small pieces, put in a bowl over a saucepan of gently simmering water and leave until soft. Stir occasionally until melted and smooth. Line a Swiss roll tin with nonstick baking parchment and pour in the melted chocolate, tilting the tin to level. Leave until set, then turn out onto a chopping board and carefully strip off the paper. Cut into 4 strips, the same length as the sponge, using a large sharp knife that has been dipped into hot water. Gently heat the apricot preserve, sieve to remove lumps and brush over the top and sides of the cake. Carefully place the chocolate strips around the cake sides and press lightly. Leave to set for at least 10 minutes.

3 For the topping, whisk the cream to soft peaks and quickly fold into the melted chocolate with the brandy. Spoon the chocolate whipped cream into a pastry bag fitted with a star nozzle and pipe a decorative design of rosettes or shells over the surface. Dust with cocoa powder and serve.

Ingredients
CUTS INTO
16 SLICES

For the chocolate sponge:
175 g/6 oz self-raising flour
1 tsp baking powder
175 g/6 oz caster sugar
175 g/6 oz butter, softened
3 large eggs
25 g/1 oz cocoa powder
150 g/5 oz apricot preserve

For the chocolate box:
275 g/10 oz dark chocolate

For the chocolate whipped cream topping:
450 ml/³/₄ pint double cream
275 g/10 oz dark chocolate, melted
2 tbsp brandy
1 tsp cocoa powder, to decorate

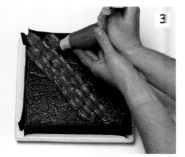

Wild Strawberry & Rose Petal Jam Cake

1   Preheat the oven to 180°C/350°F/Gas Mark 4, 10 minutes before baking. Lightly oil and flour a 20.5 cm/8 inch nonstick cake tin. Sift the flour, baking powder and salt into a bowl and reserve.

2   Beat the butter and sugar until light and fluffy. Beat in the eggs, a little at a time, then stir in the rosewater. Gently fold in the flour mixture and milk with a metal spoon or rubber spatula and mix lightly together.

3   Spoon the cake mixture into the tin, spreading evenly and smoothing the top.

4   Bake in the preheated oven for 25–30 minutes until well risen and golden and the centre springs back when pressed with a clean finger. Remove and cool, then remove from the tin.

5   For the filling, whisk the cream, yogurt, 1 tablespoon of the rosewater and 1 tablespoon icing sugar until soft peaks form. Split the cake horizontally in half and sprinkle with the remaining rosewater.

6   Spread the warmed jam on the base of the cake. Top with half the whipped cream mixture, then sprinkle with half the strawberries. Place the remaining cake half on top. Spread with the remaining cream and swirl, if desired. Decorate with the rose petals. Dust the cake lightly with a little icing sugar and serve.

Ingredients   SERVES 8

275 g/10 oz plain flour
1 tsp baking powder
1/4 tsp salt
150 g/5 oz unsalted butter, softened
200 g/7 oz caster sugar
2 large eggs, beaten
2 tbsp rosewater
125 ml/4 fl oz milk
125 g/4 oz rose petal or strawberry jam, slightly warmed
125 g/4 oz wild strawberries, hulled or baby strawberries, chopped
frosted rose petals, to decorate

For the rose cream filling:

200 ml/7 fl oz double cream
25 ml/1 fl oz natural Greek yogurt
2 tbsp rosewater
1–2 tbsp icing sugar

2

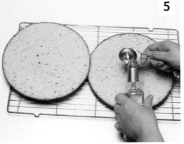

5

6

Christmas Cranberry Chocolate Log

1 Preheat the oven to 200°C/400°F/Gas Mark 6. Bring the cream to the boil over a medium heat. Remove from the heat and add all of the chocolate, stirring until melted. Stir in the brandy, if using, and strain into a medium bowl. Cool. Refrigerate for 6–8 hours.

2 Lightly oil and line a 39 x 26 cm/15¹/₂ x 10¹/₂ inch Swiss roll tin with nonstick baking parchment. Using an electric whisk, beat the egg yolks until thick and creamy. Slowly beat in the cocoa powder and half the icing sugar and reserve. Whisk the egg whites and cream of tartar into soft peaks. Gradually whisk in the remaining sugar until the mixture is stiff and glossy. Gently fold the yolk mixture into the egg whites. Spread evenly into the tin. Bake in the oven for 15 minutes. Remove and invert onto a sheet of greaseproof paper dusted with cocoa powder. Cut off the crisp edges of the cake, then roll up. Leave on a wire rack until cold.

3 For the filling, heat the cranberry sauce with the brandy, if using, until warm and spreadable. Unroll the cooled cake and spread with the cranberry sauce. Allow to cool and set. Carefully spoon the whipped cream over the surface and spread to within 2.5 cm/1 inch of the edges. Re-roll the cake. Transfer to a cake plate or tray. Allow the chocolate ganache to soften at room temperature, then beat until soft and of a spreadable consistency. Spread over the roulade and, using a fork, mark the roulade with ridges to resemble tree bark. Dust with icing sugar. Decorate with the caramelised orange strips and dried cranberries and serve.

Ingredients
CUTS INTO 12–14 SLICES

Chocolate ganache frosting
300 ml/¹/₂ pint double cream
350 g/12 oz dark chocolate, chopped
2 tbsp brandy (optional)

For the roulade:
5 large eggs, separated
3 tbsp cocoa powder, sifted, plus extra for dusting
125 g/4 oz icing sugar, sifted, plus extra for dusting
¹/₄ tsp cream of tartar

For the filling:
175 g/6 oz cranberry sauce
1–2 tbsp brandy (optional)
450 ml/³/₄ pint double cream, whipped to soft peaks

To decorate:
caramelised orange strips
dried cranberries

Christening Day Daisy Cupcakes

1 Preheat the oven to 180°C/350°F/Gas Mark 4. Line a 12–hole muffin tray with deep paper cases.

2 Place the butter and sugar in a bowl, then sift in the flour. Add the beaten eggs to the bowl with the lemon juice and milk and beat until smooth. Spoon into the cases, filling them three–quarters full.

3 Bake for about 18 minutes until firm to the touch in the centre. Turn out to cool on a wire rack.

4 To decorate, dust a clean flat surface with icing sugar. Roll out the sugarpaste thinly and stamp out daisy shapes. Leave these to dry out for 30 minutes until firm enough to handle. Pipe a small yellow gel dot into the centre of each one. Colour the frosting pale yellow, then spread onto the cakes using a palette knife. Press the daisies onto the frosting. Keep in an airtight container in a cool place for 3 days.

Ingredients   MAKES 12

150 g/5 oz butter, softened
150 g/5 oz caster sugar
150 g/5 oz self–raising flour
3 medium eggs, beaten
1 tsp lemon juice
2 tbsp milk

To decorate:
icing sugar, for dusting
125 g/4 oz sugarpaste icing
yellow gel icing tube
1 batch cream cheese frosting
   (see page 14)
yellow paste food colouring

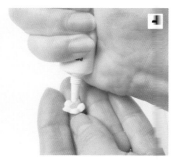

Apricot & Almond Layer Cake

1 Preheat the oven to 180°C/350°F/Gas Mark 4, 10 minutes before baking. Lightly oil and line two 23 cm/9 inch round cake tins. Cream the butter and sugar together until light and fluffy, then beat in the egg yolks, one at a time, beating well after each addition. Stir in the cooled chocolate with 1 tablespoon cooled boiled water, then fold in the flour and ground almonds.

2 Whisk the egg whites until stiff, then gradually whisk in the icing sugar, beating well after each addition. Whisk until the egg whites are stiff and glossy, then fold the egg whites into the chocolate mixture in two batches.

3 Divide the mixture evenly between the tins and bake in the oven for 30–40 minutes until firm. Leave for 5 minutes before turning out onto wire racks. Leave to cool completely.

4 Split the cakes in half. Gently heat the jam, pass through a sieve and stir in the amaretto liqueur. Place one cake layer onto a serving plate. Spread with a little of the jam, then sandwich with the next layer. Repeat with all the layers and use any remaining jam to brush over the entire cake. Leave until the jam sets.

5 Meanwhile, beat the butter and chocolate together until smooth, then cool at room temperature until thick enough to spread. Cover the top and sides of the cake with the chocolate icing and leave to set before slicing and serving.

Ingredients   SERVES 8-10

150 g/5 oz unsalted butter, softened
125 g/4 oz caster sugar
5 medium eggs, separated
150 g/5 oz dark chocolate, melted
    and cooled
150 g/5 oz self-raising flour, sifted
50 g/2 oz ground almonds
75 g/3 oz icing sugar, sifted
300 g/11 oz apricot jam
1 tbsp amaretto liqueur
125 g/4 oz unsalted butter, melted
125 g/4 oz dark chocolate, melted

Helpful Hint

Use a very good-quality apricot jam, as it is a major flavour in the finished cake

French Chocolate Pecan Torte

1 Preheat the oven to 180°C/350°F/Gas Mark 4, 10 minutes before baking. Lightly butter and line a 20.5 x 5 cm/8 x 2 inch springform tin with nonstick baking parchment. Wrap the tin in a large sheet of foil to prevent water seeping in.

2 Melt the chocolate and butter in a saucepan over a low heat and stir until smooth. Remove from the heat and cool. Using an electric whisk, beat the eggs, sugar and vanilla extract until light and foamy. Gradually beat in the melted chocolate, ground nuts and cinnamon, then pour into the tin.

3 Set the foil-wrapped tin in a large roasting tin and pour in enough boiling water to come 2 cm/³/₄ inch up the sides of the tin. Bake in the preheated oven until the edge is set but the centre is still soft when the tin is gently shaken. Remove from the oven and place on a wire rack to cool.

4 For the glaze, melt all the ingredients over a low heat until melted and smooth, then remove from the heat. Dip each pecan halfway into the glaze and set on a sheet of nonstick baking parchment until set. Allow the remaining glaze to thicken slightly.

5 Remove the cake from the tin and invert. Pour the glaze over the cake, smoothing the top and spreading the glaze around the sides. Arrange the glazed pecans around the edge of the torte. Allow to set and serve.

Ingredients   CUTS INTO 16 SLICES

200 g/7 oz dark chocolate, chopped
150 g/5 oz butter, diced
4 large eggs
100 g/3¹/₂ oz caster sugar
2 tsp vanilla extract
125 g/4 oz pecans, finely ground
2 tsp ground cinnamon
24 pecan halves, lightly toasted,
    to decorate

For the chocolate glaze:
125 g/4 oz dark chocolate, chopped
65 g/2¹/₂oz butter, diced
2 tbsp clear honey
¹/₄ tsp ground cinnamon

Food Fact
Although this recipe is French, the torte actually originates from Germany, and tends to be a very rich cake-like dessert. It is delicious served with a fruity mixed berry compote.

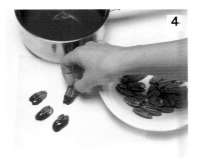

Giftwrapped Presents Cupcakes

1 Preheat the oven to 180°C/350°F/Gas Mark 4. Line one or two 12-hole muffin trays with 12–14 deep paper cases, depending on the depth of the holes.

2 Beat the butter and sugar together until light and fluffy, then beat in the eggs a little at a time, adding 1 teaspoon flour with each addition. Sift in the remaining flour and spice, add the orange zest and juice, treacle and dried fruit to the bowl and fold together until the mixture is blended.

3 Spoon into the cases and bake for about 30 minutes until firm in the centre and a skewer comes out clean. Leave to cool in the tins for 15 minutes, then turn out to cool on a wire rack. Store undecorated in an airtight container for up to 4 weeks, or freeze until needed.

4 To decorate, trim the top of each cupcake level if they have peaked, then brush with apricot glaze. Dust a clean flat surface with icing sugar. Colour the sugarpaste in batches and roll out thinly. Cut out circles 6 cm/2¹/₂ inches wide. Place a disc on top of each cupcake and press level. Mould coloured scraps into long thin sausages and roll these out thinly. Place a contrasting colour across each cupcake and arrange into bows and loops. Leave to dry for 24 hours if possible. Keep for 4 days in an airtight container.

Ingredients   MAKES 12–14

125 g/4 oz butter, softened
125 g/4 oz soft dark
    muscovado sugar
2 medium eggs, beaten
225 g/8 oz self-raising flour
1 tsp ground mixed spice
finely grated zest and 1 tbsp juice
    from 1 orange
1 tbsp black treacle
350 g/12 oz mixed dried fruit

To decorate:

3 tbsp sieved apricot glaze (see
    page 15)
icing sugar, for dusting
600 g/1 lb 5 oz ready-to-roll
    sugarpaste
red, blue, green and yellow paste
    food colourings

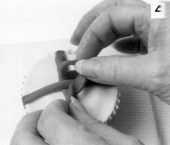

Double Marble Cake

1 Preheat the oven to 180˚C/350˚F/Gas Mark 4, 10 minutes before baking. Lightly oil and line the base of a 20.5 cm/8 inch cake tin. Break the white and dark chocolate into small pieces, then place in two separate bowls placed over two pans of simmering water, ensuring that the bowls are not touching the water. Heat the chocolate until melted and smooth.

2 In a large bowl, cream the sugar and butter together until light and fluffy. Beat in the egg yolks one at a time and add a spoonful of flour after each addition. Stir in the ground almonds. In another bowl, whisk the egg whites until stiff. Gently fold in the egg whites and the remaining sifted flour alternately into the almond mixture until all the flour and egg whites have been incorporated. Divide the mixture between two bowls. Gently stir the white chocolate into one bowl, then add the dark chocolate to the other bowl. Place alternating spoonfuls of the chocolate mixtures in the cake tin. Using a skewer, swirl the mixtures together to get a marbled effect, then tap the tin on the work surface to level the mixture. Bake in the oven for 40 minutes, or until cooked through, then leave to cool for 5 minutes in the tin before turning out onto a wire rack to cool completely.

3 For the topping, melt half of the cream and butter with the dark chocolate and the other half with the white chocolate and stir both until smooth. Cool, then whisk until thick and swirl both colours over the top of the cake to create a marbled effect.

Ingredients
CUTS INTO
8–10 SLICES

75 g/3 oz white chocolate
75 g/3 oz dark chocolate
175 g/6 oz caster sugar
175 g/6 oz butter
4 medium eggs, separated
125 g/4 oz plain flour, sifted
75 g/3 oz ground almonds

For the topping:
100 ml/4 fl oz double cream
200 g/7 oz unsalted butter
100 g/3^1/$_2$ oz dark chocolate, chopped
100 g/3^1/$_2$ oz white chocolate, chopped

Orange Fruit Cake

1
Preheat the oven to 180°C/350°F/Gas Mark 4, 10 minutes before baking. Lightly oil and line the base of a 25.5 cm/10 inch deep cake tin or springform tin with nonstick baking parchment.

2
Sift the flour and baking powder into a large bowl and stir in the sugar. Make a well in the centre and add the butter, eggs, grated zest and orange juice. Beat until blended and a smooth batter is formed. Turn into the tin and smooth the top.

3
Bake in the oven for 35–45 minutes, or until golden and the sides begin to shrink from the edge of the tin. Remove, cool before removing from the tin and discard the lining paper. Using a serrated knife, slice off the top third off cake, cutting horizontally. Sprinkle the cut sides with the Cointreau.

4
To make the filling, whip the cream and yogurt with the vanilla extract, Cointreau and icing sugar until soft peaks form. Chop the orange fruit and fold into the cream. Spread some of this mixture onto the bottom cake layer. Transfer to a serving plate.

5
Cover with the top layer of sponge and spread the remaining cream mixture over the top and sides. Press the chopped nuts into the sides of the cake and decorate the top with the Cape gooseberries, blueberries, raspberries and mint. If liked, dust the top with icing sugar and serve.

Ingredients
CUTS INTO
10–12 SLICES

For the orange cake:
225 g/8 oz self-raising flour
2 tsp baking powder
225 g/8 oz caster sugar
225 g/8 oz butter, softened
4 large eggs
grated zest of 1 orange
2 tbsp orange juice
2–3 tbsp Cointreau
125 g/4 oz chopped nuts
Cape gooseberries, blueberries, raspberries, mint sprigs, to decorate
icing sugar, for dusting (optional)

For the filling:
450 ml/³/₄ pint double cream
50 ml/2 fl oz Greek yogurt
¹/₂ tsp vanilla extract
2–3 tbsp Cointreau
1 tbsp icing sugar
450 g/1 lb orange fruits, such as mango, peach, nectarine, papaya and yellow plums

Rich Devil's Food Cake

1 Preheat the oven to 180°C/350°F/Gas Mark 4, 10 minutes before baking. Lightly oil and line the bases of three 23 cm/9 inch cake tins with greaseproof or baking paper. Sift the flour, salt and bicarbonate of soda into a bowl. Sift the cocoa powder into another bowl. Gradually whisk in a little of the milk to form a paste. Continue whisking in the milk until it is a smooth mixture.

2 Beat the butter, sugar and vanilla extract until light and fluffy then gradually beat in the eggs, beating well after each addition. Stir in the flour and cocoa mixtures alternately in three or four batches. Divide the mixture evenly among the three tins, smoothing the surfaces evenly. Bake in the oven for 25–35 minutes until cooked and firm to the touch. Remove, cool and turn out onto a wire rack. Discard the lining paper.

3 To make the frosting, put the sugar, salt and chocolate into a heavy-based saucepan. Stir in the milk until blended. Add the golden syrup and butter. Bring the mixture to the boil over a medium-high heat, stirring to help dissolve the sugar. Boil for 1 minute, stirring constantly. Remove from the heat, stir in the vanilla extract and cool, then whisk until thickened and slightly lightened in colour. Sandwich the three cake layers together with about a third of the frosting, placing the third cake layer with the flat side up. Transfer the cake to a serving plate and spread the remaining frosting over the top and sides. Swirl the top to create a decorative effect and serve.

Ingredients

CUTS INTO
12–16 SLICES

450 g/1 lb plain flour
$^1/_2$ tsp salt
1 tbsp bicarbonate of soda
75 g/3 oz cocoa powder
300 ml/$^1/_2$ pint milk
150 g/5 oz butter, softened
400 g/14 oz soft dark brown sugar
2 tsp vanilla extract
4 large eggs

For the chocolate fudge frosting:

275 g/10 oz caster sugar
$^1/_2$ tsp salt
125 g/4 oz dark chocolate, chopped
225 ml/8 fl oz milk
2 tbsp golden syrup
125 g/4 oz butter, diced
2 tsp vanilla extract

Mocha Truffle Cake

1 Preheat the oven to 180°C/350°F/Gas Mark 4, 10 minutes before cooking. Lightly oil and line a deep 23 cm/9 inch round cake tin. Beat the eggs and sugar in a bowl until thick and creamy. Sift together the cornflour, self-raising flour and cocoa powder and fold lightly into the egg mixture. Spoon into the tin and bake in the oven for 30 minutes, or until firm. Turn out onto a wire rack and leave until cold. Split the cold cake horizontally into two layers. Mix together the milk and coffee liqueur and brush onto the cake layers.

2 Stir the cooled white chocolate into one bowl and the cooled dark chocolate into another one. Whip the cream until soft peaks form, then divide between the two bowls and stir. Place one layer of cake in a 23 cm/9 inch springform tin. Spread with half the white chocolate cream. Top with the dark chocolate cream, then the remaining white chocolate cream. Finally, place the remaining cake layer on top. Chill in the refrigerator for 4 hours, or overnight, until set.

3 When ready to serve, melt the milk chocolate and butter in a heatproof bowl set over a saucepan of simmering water and stir until smooth. Remove from the heat and leave until thick enough to spread, then use to cover the top and sides of the cake. Leave to set at room temperature, then chill in the refrigerator. Cut the cake into slices and serve.

Ingredients

CUTS INTO 8-10 SLICES

3 medium eggs

125 g/4 oz caster sugar

40 g/1½ oz cornflour

40 g/1½ oz self-raising flour

2 tbsp cocoa powder

2 tbsp milk

2 tbsp coffee liqueur

100 g/3½ oz white chocolate, melted and cooled

200 g/7 oz dark chocolate, melted and cooled

600 ml/1 pint double cream

200 g/7 oz milk chocolate

100 g/3½ oz unsalted butter

Helpful Hint

Unless you are going to make a lot of chocolate or coffee desserts, liqueurs are very expensive to buy. Look for supermarket own-label brands or miniatures.

Italian Polenta Cake with Mascarpone Cream

1 Preheat the oven to 190°C/375°F/Gas Mark 5, 10 minutes before baking. Butter a 23 cm/9 inch springform tin. Dust lightly with flour. Stir the flour, polenta or cornmeal, baking powder, salt and lemon zest together. Beat the eggs and half the sugar until light and fluffy. Slowly beat in the milk and almond extract.

2 Stir in the raisins or sultanas, then beat in the flour mixture and 50 g/2 oz of the butter. Spoon into the tin and smooth the top evenly. Arrange the pear slices on top in overlapping concentric circles.

3 Melt the remaining butter and brush over the pear slices. Sprinkle with the rest of the sugar. Bake in the preheated oven for about 40 minutes until puffed and golden and the edges of the pears are lightly caramelised. Transfer to a wire rack. Reserve to cool in the tin for 15 minutes. Remove the cake from the tin. Heat the apricot jam with 1 tablespoon water and brush over the top of the cake to glaze.

4 Beat the mascarpone cheese with the sugar to taste, the cream and amaretto or rum until smooth and forming a soft dropping consistency. Serve with the polenta cake. When cool, sprinkle the almonds over the polenta cake and dust generously with the icing sugar. Serve the cake with the liqueur–flavoured mascarpone cream on the side.

Ingredients

CUTS INTO
6–8 SLICES

1 tsp butter and flour for the tin
100 g/3½ oz plain flour
40 g/1½ oz polenta or
   yellow cornmeal
1 tsp baking powder
¼ tsp salt
grated zest of 1 lemon
2 large eggs
150 g/5 oz caster sugar
5 tbsp milk
½ tsp almond extract
2 tbsp raisins or sultanas
75 g/3 oz unsalted butter, softened
2 medium dessert pears, peeled,
   cored and thinly sliced
2 tbsp apricot jam
175 g/6 oz mascarpone cheese
1–2 tsp sugar
50 ml/2 fl oz double cream
2 tbsp amaretto liqueur or rum
2–3 tbsp toasted flaked almonds
icing sugar, for dusting

Almond Angel Cake with Amaretto Cream

1 Preheat the oven to 180°C/350°F/Gas Mark 4, 10 minutes before baking. Sift together the 175 g/6 oz icing sugar and flour. Stir to blend, then sift again and reserve. Using an electric whisk, beat the egg whites, cream of tartar, vanilla extract , $^1/_2$ teaspoon of the almond extract and salt on medium speed until soft peaks form. Gradually add the caster sugar, 2 tablespoons at a time, beating well after each addition, until stiff peaks form.

2 Sift about one third of the flour mixture over the egg white mixture and gently fold in. Repeat, folding the flour mixture into the egg white mixture in two more batches. Spoon gently into an ungreased angel food cake tin or 25.5 cm/10 inch tube tin. Bake in the oven until risen and golden on top and the surface springs back quickly when gently pressed with a clean finger. Immediately invert the cake tin and cool completely in the tin.

3 When cool, carefully run a sharp knife around the edge of the tin and the centre ring to loosen the cake from the edge. Using the fingertips, ease the cake from the tin and invert onto a cake plate. Thickly dust the cake with the extra icing sugar. Whip the cream with the remaining almond extract, liqueur and a little more icing sugar until soft peaks form. Fill a piping bag fitted with a star nozzle with half the cream and pipe around the bottom edge of the cake. Decorate the edge with the fresh raspberries and serve the remaining cream separately.

Ingredients
CUTS INTO 10–12 SLICES

175 g/6 oz icing sugar, plus 2–3 tbsp
150 g/5 oz plain flour
350 ml/12 fl oz egg whites (about 10 large egg whites)
1$^1/_2$ tsp cream of tartar
$^1/_2$ tsp vanilla extract
1 tsp almond extract
$^1/_4$ tsp salt
200 g/7 oz caster sugar
175 ml/6 fl oz double cream
2 tbsp amaretto liqueur
fresh raspberries, to decorate

Food Fact
Angel cake has a very light and delicate texture, and can be difficult to slice. For best results, use two forks to gently separate a portion of the cake.

Chocolate Mousse Sponge

1 Preheat the oven to 180°C/350°F/Gas Mark 4, 10 minutes before baking. Lightly oil and line a 23 cm/9 inch round cake tin and lightly oil the sides of a 23 cm/9 inch springform tin. Whisk the eggs, sugar and vanilla extract until thick and creamy. Fold in the flour, ground almonds and dark chocolate. Spoon the mixture into the prepared round cake tin and bake in the preheated oven for 25 minutes, or until firm. Turn out onto a wire rack to cool.

2 For the mousse, soak the gelatine in 50 ml/2 fl oz cold water for 5 minutes until softened. Meanwhile, heat the double cream in a small saucepan. When almost boiling, remove from the heat and stir in the chocolate and vanilla extract . Stir until the chocolate melts. Squeeze the excess water out of the gelatine and add to the chocolate mixture. Stir until dissolved, then pour into a large bowl.

3 Whisk the egg whites until stiff, then gradually add the caster sugar, whisking well after each addition. Fold the egg white mixture into the chocolate mixture in two batches. Split the cake into two layers. Place one layer in the bottom of the springform tin. Pour in the mousse mixture, then top with the second layer of cake. Chill in the refrigerator for 4 hours, or until the mousse has set. Loosen the sides and remove the cake from the tin. Dust with icing sugar and decorate the top with a few freshly sliced strawberries. Serve cut into slices.

Ingredients

CUTS INTO
8–10 SLICES

3 medium eggs
75 g/3 oz caster sugar
1 tsp vanilla extract
50 g/2 oz self-raising flour, sifted
25 g/1 oz ground almonds
50 g/2 oz dark chocolate, grated
icing sugar, for dusting
freshly sliced strawberries, to decorate

For the mousse:

2 sheets gelatine
50 ml/2 fl oz double cream
100 g/3$\frac{1}{2}$ oz dark chocolate, chopped
1 tsp vanilla extract
4 medium egg whites
125 g/4 oz caster sugar

Tasty Tip

Sheet gelatine is very easy to use. Soak the gelatine as described in step 2, then squeeze out the excess liquid. It must then be added to hot liquid where it will melt on contact.

Buttery Passion Fruit Madeira Cake

1 Preheat the oven to 180°C/350°F/Gas Mark 4, 10 minutes before baking. Lightly oil and line the base of a 23 x 12.5 cm/ 9 x 5 inch loaf tin with greaseproof paper. Sift the flour and baking powder into a bowl and reserve.

2 Beat the butter, sugar, orange zest and vanilla extract until light and fluffy, then gradually beat in the eggs, 1 tablespoon at a time, beating well after each addition. If the mixture appears to curdle or separate, beat in a little of the flour mixture.

3 Fold in the flour mixture with the milk until just blended. Do not overmix. Spoon lightly into the prepared tin and smooth the top evenly. Sprinkle lightly with the teaspoon of caster sugar.

4 Bake in the oven for 55 minutes, or until well risen and golden brown. Remove from the oven and leave to cool for 15–20 minutes. Cut the passion fruit in half and scoop out the pulp into a sieve set over a bowl. Press the juice through using a rubber spatula or wooden spoon. Stir in the icing sugar and stir to dissolve, adding a little extra sugar if necessary.

5 Using a skewer, pierce holes all over the cake. Slowly spoon the passion fruit glaze over the cake and allow to seep in. Gently turn the cake out of the tin onto a wire rack and turn it back the right way up, discarding the lining paper. Dust with icing sugar and cool completely. Serve the Madeira cake cold.

Ingredients CUTS INTO 8-10 SLICES

210 g/7¹/₂ oz plain flour
1 tsp baking powder
175 g/6 oz unsalted
    butter, softened
250 g/9 oz caster sugar, plus 1 tsp
grated zest of 1 orange
1 tsp vanilla extract
3 medium eggs, beaten
2 tbsp milk
6 ripe passion fruit
50 g/2 oz icing sugar
icing sugar, for dusting

Food Fact

Regardless of its name, Madeira cake does not actually originate from the Portuguese–owned island of Madeira. It is, in fact, a traditional English favourite which acquired its name because the cake was often served with the fortified wine, Madeira.

3

4

5

Chocolate Roulade

1 Preheat the oven to 180°C/350°F/Gas Mark 4, 10 minutes before baking. Lightly oil and line a 33 cm x 23 cm/13 inch x 9 inch Swiss roll tin with nonstick baking parchment. Break the chocolate into small pieces into a heatproof bowl set over a saucepan of simmering water. Leave until almost melted, stirring occasionally. Remove from the heat and leave to stand for 5 minutes.

2 Whisk the egg yolks with the sugar until pale and creamy and the whisk leaves a trail in the mixture when lifted, then carefully fold in the melted chocolate. In a clean grease-free bowl, whisk the egg whites until stiff, then fold 1 large spoonful into the chocolate mixture. Mix lightly, then gently fold in the remaining egg whites. Pour the mixture into the tin and level the surface. Bake in the oven for 20–25 minutes until firm.

3 Remove the cake from the oven, leave in the tin and cover with a wire rack and a damp tea towel. Leave for 8 hours, or preferably overnight. Dust a large sheet of nonstick baking parchment with 2 tablespoons of the icing sugar. Unwrap the cake and turn out onto the greaseproof paper. Remove the baking parchment. Whip the cream with the liqueur until soft peaks form. Spread over the cake, leaving a 2.5 cm/1 inch border all round.

4 Using the paper, roll the cake up from a short end. Transfer to a serving plate, seam-side down, and dust with the remaining icing sugar. Decorate with fresh raspberries and mint. Serve.

Ingredients   CUTS INTO
8 SLICES

200 g/7 oz dark chocolate
7 medium eggs, separated
200 g/7 oz caster sugar
300 ml/¹/₂ pint double cream
3 tbsp Cointreau or Grand Marnier
4 tbsp icing sugar, for dusting

To decorate:
fresh raspberries
fresh mint sprigs

Tasty Tip
Leaving the cake in the tin overnight gives it a fudgy texture and also means that the cake is less likely to break when it is rolled up.

Cakes for Afternoon Tea

Add a little decadence to your afternoon. Pair Cappuccino Cakes with a pot of coffee or a slice of Sauternes and Olive Oil Cake with a cup of tea for a fabulous break from your day. These cakes are so good that you'll be reaching for another slice in no time!

Pineapple, Cream Cheese & Carrot Muffins

1 Preheat the oven to 180°C/350°F/Gas Mark 4. Lightly oil a deep 12-hole muffin tray or line with deep paper cases. Chop the soft dried pineapple and set aside.

2 Sift the flour, baking powder, cinnamon and salt into a bowl, including any bran from the sieve. Add the oil, sugar, eggs, chopped pineapple and grated carrots.

3 Beat until smooth, then spoon into the muffin cases. Bake for 20–25 minutes until risen and golden. Cool on a wire rack.

4 To decorate the muffins, beat the cream cheese and icing sugar together with the lemon juice to make a spreading consistency. Swirl the icing over the top of each cupcake, then top with a piece of pineapple. If chilled and sealed in an airtight container, these will keep for 3–4 days.

Ingredients   MAKES 12

50 g/2 oz soft dried pineapple
175 g/6 oz self-raising wholemeal flour
1 tsp baking powder
$^1/_2$ tsp ground cinnamon
pinch salt
150 ml/$^1/_4$ pint sunflower oil
150 g/5 oz soft light brown sugar
3 medium eggs, beaten
225 g/8 oz carrots, peeled and
    finely grated

To decorate:

75 g/3 oz cream cheese
175 g/6 oz golden icing sugar
2 tsp lemon juice
50 g/2 oz soft dried pineapple
    pieces, thinly sliced

Rich Chocolate Cupcakes

1 Preheat the oven to 180°C/350°F/Gas Mark 4, 10 minutes before baking. Line a 12-hole muffin tin or deep bun tray with paper muffin cases. Sift the flour and cocoa powder into a bowl. Stir in the sugar, then add the melted butter, eggs and vanilla extract. Beat together with a wooden spoon for 3 minutes, or until well blended.

2 Divide half the mixture between six of the paper cases. Dry the cherries thoroughly on absorbent kitchen paper, then fold into the remaining mixture and spoon into the rest of the paper cases.

3 Bake on the shelf above the centre of the preheated oven for 20 minutes, or until a skewer inserted into the centre of a cake comes out clean. Transfer to a wire rack and leave to cool.

4 For the chocolate icing, melt the chocolate and butter in a heatproof bowl set over a saucepan of simmering water. Remove from the heat and leave to cool for 3 minutes, stirring occasionally. Stir in the icing sugar. Spoon over the six plain chocolate cakes and leave to set.

5 For the cherry icing, sift the icing sugar into a bowl and stir in 1 tablespoon boiling water, the butter and cherry syrup. Spoon the icing over the remaining six cakes, decorate each with a halved cherry and leave to set.

Ingredients MAKES 2

175 g/6 oz self-raising flour
25 g/1 oz cocoa powder
175 g/6 oz soft light brown sugar
75 g/3 oz butter, melted
2 medium eggs, lightly beaten
1 tsp vanilla extract
40 g/1^1/$_2$ oz maraschino cherries, drained and chopped

For the chocolate icing:
50 g/2 oz dark chocolate
25 g/1 oz unsalted butter
25 g/1 oz icing sugar, sifted

For the cherry icing:
125 g/4 oz icing sugar
7 g/^{1}/$_4$ oz unsalted butter, melted
1 tsp syrup from the maraschino cherries
3 maraschino cherries, halved, to decorate

Moist Mocha & Coconut Cake

1 Preheat the oven to 170°C/325°F/Gas Mark 3, 10 minutes before baking. Lightly oil and line a deep 20.5 cm/8 inch square tin with nonstick baking parchment. Place the ground coffee in a small bowl and pour over the hot milk. Leave to infuse for 5 minutes, then strain through a tea strainer or a sieve lined with muslin. You will end up with about 4 tablespoons of liquid. Reserve.

2 Put the butter, golden syrup, sugar and coconut in a small heavy-based saucepan and heat gently until the butter has melted and the sugar dissolved. Sift the flour, cocoa powder and bicarbonate of soda together and stir into the melted mixture with the eggs and 3 tablespoons of the coffee-infused milk.

3 Pour the mixture into the prepared tin. Bake on the centre shelf of the preheated oven for 45 minutes, or until the cake is well risen and firm to the touch. Leave in the tin for 10 minutes to cool slightly, then turn out onto a wire rack to cool completely.

4 For the icing, gradually add the icing sugar to the softened butter and beat together until mixed. Add the remaining 1 tablespoon of the coffee-infused milk and beat until light and fluffy.

5 Carefully spread the coffee icing over the top of the cake, then cut into 9 squares. Decorate each square with a small piece of chocolate flake and serve.

Ingredients

MAKES
9 SQUARES

3 tbsp ground coffee
5 tbsp hot milk
75 g/3 oz butter
175 g/6 oz golden syrup
25 g/1 oz soft light brown sugar
40 g/1$\frac{1}{2}$ oz desiccated coconut
150 g/5 oz plain flour
25 g/1 oz cocoa powder
$\frac{1}{2}$ tsp bicarbonate of soda
2 medium eggs, lightly beaten
3 chocolate flakes, to decorate

For the coffee icing:
225 g/8 oz icing sugar, sifted
125 g/4 oz butter, softened

Helpful Hint
It is important to use a very fine strainer to remove as much of the coffee as possible, or the cake will have an unpleasant gritty texture.

Fudgy & Top Hat Chocolate Buns

1 Preheat the oven to 190°C/375°F/Gas Mark 5, 10 minutes before baking. Sift the flour, cocoa powder and baking powder into a bowl. Add the butter, sugar, egg and milk. Beat for 2–3 minutes until light and fluffy.

2 Divide the mixture equally between 12 paper cases arranged in a bun tray. Bake on the shelf above the centre in the preheated oven for 15–20 minutes until well risen and firm to the touch. Leave in the bun tray for a few minutes, then transfer to a wire rack and leave to cool completely.

3 For the fudgy icing, mix together the melted butter, milk, cocoa powder and icing sugar. Place a spoonful of icing on the top of six of the buns, spreading out to a circle with the back of the spoon. Sprinkle with grated chocolate.

4 To make the top hats, use a sharp knife to cut and remove a circle of sponge, about 3 cm/1¹/₄ inches across from each of the six remaining cakes. Whip the cream, orange liqueur and icing sugar together until soft peaks form.

5 Spoon the filling into a piping bag fitted with a large star nozzle and pipe a swirl in the centre of each cake. Replace the tops, then dust with the remaining icing sugar and serve with the other buns.

Ingredients   MAKES 12

50 g/2 oz self-raising flour
25 g/1 oz cocoa powder
¹/₂ tsp baking powder
75 g/3 oz butter, softened
75 g/3 oz soft light brown sugar
1 medium egg, lightly beaten
1 tbsp milk

For the fudgy icing:

15 g/¹/₂ oz unsalted butter, melted
1 tbsp milk
15 g/¹/₂ oz cocoa powder, sifted
40 g/1¹/₂ oz icing sugar, sifted
25 g/1 oz dark chocolate, coarsely
   grated

For the top hat filling:

150 ml/¹/₄ pint whipping cream
2 tsp orange liqueur
1 tbsp icing sugar, sifted

Toffee Walnut Swiss Roll

1 Preheat the oven to 190°C/375°F/Gas Mark 5, 10 minutes before baking. Lightly oil and line a Swiss roll tin with nonstick baking parchment. Beat the egg whites and cream of tartar until softly peaking. Gradually beat in 50 g/2 oz of the icing sugar until stiff peaks form. In another bowl, beat the egg yolks with the remaining icing sugar until thick. Beat in the vanilla extract. Gently fold in the flour and egg whites alternately using a metal spoon or rubber spatula. Do not overmix. Spoon into the tin and spread evenly. Bake in the oven for 12 minutes, or until well risen, golden and the cake springs back when pressed with a clean finger. Lay a clean tea towel on a work surface, lay a piece of baking parchment about 33 cm/13 inches long on it and dust with icing sugar. As soon as the cake is cooked, turn out onto the paper. Peel off the lining paper and cut off the crisp edges of the cake. Starting at one narrow end, roll the cake with the paper and towel. Transfer to a wire rack and cool completely.

2 For the filling, put the flour, milk and syrup into a small saucepan and place over a gentle heat. Bring to the boil, whisking until thick and smooth. Remove from the heat and slowly beat into the beaten egg yolks. Pour back into the saucepan and cook over a low heat until it thickens and coats the back of a spoon. Strain into a bowl and stir in the chopped nuts. Cool, stirring occasionally, then fold in about half of the whipped cream. Unroll the cooled cake and spread the filling over it. Re-roll and decorate with the remaining cream. Sprinkle with the icing sugar and serve.

Ingredients
CUTS INTO 10–12 SLICES

4 large eggs, separated
$^1/_2$ tsp cream of tartar
125 g/4 oz icing sugar, plus extra
    for dusting
$^1/_2$ tsp vanilla extract
125 g/4 oz self-raising flour

For the toffee walnut filling:
2 tbsp plain flour
150 ml/$^1/_4$ pint milk
5 tbsp golden syrup or maple syrup
2 large egg yolks, beaten
100 g/3$^1/_2$ oz walnuts or pecans,
    toasted and chopped
300 ml/$^1/_2$ pint double
    cream, whipped

Food Fact
Using a clean tea towel to roll up the sponge in this recipe turns the steam into condensation which helps to keep the cake fairly flexible and therefore prevents it from cracking.

Chocolate & Orange Rock Buns

1 Preheat the oven to 200°C/400°F/Gas Mark 6, 15 minutes before baking. Lightly oil two baking sheets, or line them with nonstick baking parchment. Sift the flour, cocoa powder and baking powder into a bowl. Cut the butter into small squares. Add to the dry ingredients, then, using your hands, rub in until the mixture resembles fine breadcrumbs.

2 Add the granulated sugar, pineapple, apricots and cherries to the bowl and stir to mix. Lightly beat the egg together with the grated orange zest and juice. Drizzle the egg mixture over the dry ingredients and stir to combine. The mixture should be fairly stiff but not too dry; add a little more orange juice, if needed.

3 Using two teaspoons, shape the mixture into 12 rough heaps on the prepared baking sheets. Sprinkle generously with the demerara sugar. Bake in the preheated oven for 15 minutes, switching the baking sheets around after 10 minutes. Leave on the baking sheets for 5 minutes to cool slightly, then transfer to a wire rack to cool. Serve warm or cold.

Ingredients   MAKES 12

200 g/7 oz self-raising flour
25 g/1 oz cocoa powder
$^{1}/_{2}$ tsp baking powder
125 g/4 oz butter
40 g/1$^{1}/_{2}$ oz granulated sugar
50 g/2 oz candied pineapple, chopped
50 g/2 oz ready-to-eat dried
    apricots, chopped
50 g/2 oz glacé cherries, quartered
1 medium egg
finely grated zest of $^{1}/_{2}$ orange
1 tbsp orange juice
2 tbsp demerara sugar

Helpful Hint

It is important not to overmix the ingredients or add too much liquid, otherwise the 'rocky' texture of the buns will be lost. Vary the ingredients according to personal preference. These buns are best eaten within a day of being made, as they do not keep very well.

1

2

3

Coconut & Lime Muffins

1 Preheat the oven to 180°C/350°F/Gas Mark 4. Line a deep 12-hole muffin tray with deep paper cases.

2 Place the margarine and caster sugar in a bowl and add the eggs and coconut. Finely grate the zest from the lime into the bowl, then squeeze in the juice. Sift in the flour and baking powder.

3 Add the milk and whisk together for about 2 minutes with an electric beater, or by hand until smooth, then spoon into the paper cases. Bake for 15–20 minutes until golden and firm. Cool on a wire rack.

4 To decorate the muffins, beat the butter and icing sugar together until smooth, then pipe or swirl onto each muffin. Press the coconut chips into the buttercream and then scatter the grated lime zest on top. Keep for 3 days in an airtight container in a cool place.

Ingredients MAKES 2

125 g/4 oz soft margarine
125 g/4 oz golden caster sugar
2 medium eggs
50 g/2 oz desiccated coconut
1 lime
125 g/4 oz self-raising flour
1 tsp baking powder
2 tbsp milk

To decorate:
40 g/1½ oz unsalted butter
125 g/4 oz icing sugar
50 g/2 oz coconut chips
zest of 1 lime, grated

Banana & Honey Tea Bread

1 Preheat the oven to 180°C/350°F/Gas Mark 4. Grease a 900 g/ 2 lb loaf tin and line the base with a strip of nonstick baking parchment. Mash the bananas together in a large bowl with the orange juice.

2 Place the soft margarine, sugar and honey in the bowl and add the eggs. Sift in the flour and cinnamon, adding any bran left behind in the sieve. Beat everything together until light and fluffy and then fold in the sultanas.

3 Spoon the mixture into the prepared tin and smooth the top to make it level. Bake for about 1 hour until golden, well risen and a skewer inserted into the centre comes out clean.

4 Cool in the tin for 5 minutes, then turn out on a wire rack.

Ingredients
MAKES ONE
900 G/2 LB LOAF

2 large peeled bananas,
    about 225 g/8 oz
1 tbsp fresh orange juice
125 g/4 oz soft margarine
125 g/4 oz soft light
    brown sugar
125 g/4 oz honey
2 medium eggs, beaten
225 g/8 oz wholemeal self–raising
    flour
$1/2$ tsp ground cinnamon
75 g/3 oz sultanas

Chocolate Madeleines

1 Preheat the oven to 180°C/350°F/Gas Mark 4, 10 minutes before baking. Lightly oil 10 dariole moulds and line the bases of each with a small circle of nonstick baking parchment. Stand the moulds on a baking tray. Cream the butter and sugar together until light and fluffy. Gradually add the eggs, beating well between each addition. Beat in the almond extract and ground almonds.

2 Sift the flour, cocoa powder and baking powder over the creamed mixture. Gently fold in using a metal spoon. Divide the mixture equally between the prepared moulds; each should be about half full.

3 Bake on the centre shelf of the preheated oven for 20 minutes, or until well risen and firm to the touch. Leave in the tins for a few minutes, then run a small palette knife round the edge and turn out onto a wire rack to cool. Remove the paper circles from the sponges.

4 Heat the conserve with the liqueur, brandy or juice in a small saucepan. Sieve to remove any lumps. If necessary, trim the sponge bases so they are flat. Brush the tops and sides with warm conserve, then roll in the coconut. Top each with a chocolate button, fixed by brushing its base with conserve.

Ingredients   MAKES 10

125 g/4 oz butter
125 g/4 oz soft light brown sugar
2 medium eggs, lightly beaten
1 drop almond extract
1 tbsp ground almonds
75 g/3 oz self-raising flour
20 g/^{3}/$_4$ oz cocoa powder
1 tsp baking powder

To decorate:
5 tbsp apricot conserve
1 tbsp amaretto liqueur, brandy or
    orange juice
50 g/2 oz desiccated coconut
10 large chocolate buttons (optional)

Helpful Hint
Oil the tins well and, if liked, dust with a little flour, shaking off any excess flour. Remove the madeleines as soon as possible after baking, as they have a tendency to stick.

Tropical Mango Muffins

1 Preheat the oven to 200°C/400°F/Gas Mark 6. Line a deep muffin tray with 10 deep paper muffin cases. Wet a sharp knife and chop the fruits into small chunks. Set them aside.

2 Sift the flour, baking powder and bicarbonate of soda into a large bowl. Add the sugar and make a well in the centre. In another bowl, beat the egg and milk together with the orange juice.

3 Add the milk to the bowl with the melted butter and the orange zest and beat with a fork until all the flour is combined but the mixture is still slightly lumpy. Fold in three quarters of the chopped fruit and spoon into the paper cases. Sprinkle the remaining fruit over the top of each muffin.

4 Bake for about 20 minutes until risen, golden and firm. Cool on a wire rack and eat warm or cold. Keep for 24 hours sealed in an airtight container.

Ingredients

CUTS INTO
8–10 SLICES

50 g/2 oz soft dried pineapple chunks
50 g/2 oz soft dried papaya pieces
25 g/1 oz soft dried mango pieces
225 g/8 oz plain flour
1 tsp baking powder
$^1/_2$ tsp bicarbonate of soda
75 g/3 oz golden caster sugar
1 medium egg
275 ml/9 fl oz milk
zest and 1 tbsp juice from 1 small orange
50 g/2 oz butter, melted and cooled

Lemony Coconut Cake

1 Preheat the oven to 180°C/350°F/Gas Mark 4, 10 minutes before baking. Lightly oil and flour two 20.5 cm/8 inch nonstick cake tins. Sift the flour, cornflour, baking powder and salt into a large bowl and add the white vegetable fat or margarine, sugar, lemon zest, vanilla extract, eggs and milk. With an electric whisk on a low speed, beat until blended, adding a little extra milk if the mixture is very stiff. Increase the speed to medium and beat for about 2 minutes.

2 Divide the mixture between the tins and smooth the tops evenly. Bake in the oven for 20–25 minutes until the cakes feel firm and are cooked. Remove from the oven and cool before removing from the tins.

3 Put all the frosting ingredients, except the coconut, into a heatproof bowl placed over a saucepan of simmering water. Using an electric whisk, blend the frosting ingredients on a low speed. Increase the speed to high and beat for 7 minutes until the whites are stiff and glossy. Remove the bowl from the heat and continue beating until cool. Cover with clingfilm.

4 Using a serrated knife, split the cake layers horizontally in half and sprinkle each cut surface with the Malibu or rum. Sandwich the cakes together with the lemon curd and press lightly. Spread the top and sides generously with the frosting, swirling and peaking the top. Sprinkle the coconut over the top of the cake and gently press onto the sides to cover. Decorate with the lime zest. Serve.

Ingredients
CUTS INTO
10–12 SLICES

275 g/10 oz plain flour
2 tbsp cornflour
1 tbsp baking powder
1 tsp salt
150 g/5 oz white vegetable fat
   or soft margarine
275 g/10 oz caster sugar
grated zest of 2 lemons
1 tsp vanilla extract
3 large eggs
150 ml/$\frac{1}{4}$ pint milk
4 tbsp Malibu or rum
450 g/1 lb jar lemon curd
lime zest, to decorate

For the frosting:
275 g/10 oz caster sugar
125 ml/4 fl oz water
1 tbsp glucose
$\frac{1}{4}$ tsp salt
1 tsp vanilla extract
3 large egg whites
75 g/3 oz desiccated coconut

1

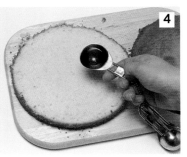
4

4

Butterscotch Loaf

1 Preheat the oven to 170°C/325°F/Gas Mark 3. Grease and line the base of a 1 kg/2 lb loaf tin with a long thin strip of nonstick baking parchment.

2 Place the banana in a bowl and mash. Add the margarine, sugar and eggs along with the extracts and sift in the flour. Beat until smooth, then stir in the chocolate chips and add half the chopped walnuts. Stir until smooth, then spoon into the tin and spread level.

3 Bake for about 45 minutes until a skewer inserted into the centre comes out clean. Leave in the tin for 5 minutes, then turn out onto a wire rack, peel away the paper and leave to cool.

4 To decorate, add 2 teaspoons water to the icing sugar and make into a runny consistency. Drizzle over the cake and sprinkle over the remaining walnuts and the sugar lumps. Leave to set for 30 minutes, then serve sliced.

Ingredients   SERVES 8

1 banana, peeled, weighing about
    100 g/3$^1/_2$ oz
125 g/4 oz soft margarine
125 g/4 oz golden caster sugar
2 medium eggs
1 tsp almond extract
$^1/_2$ tsp vanilla extract
125 g/4 oz self-raising flour
75 g/3 oz dark chocolate chips
75 g/3 oz walnuts, chopped

To decorate:
50 g/2 oz natural icing sugar
25 g/1 oz golden lump sugar,
    chopped

Blackcurrant & Lemon Muffins

1 Preheat the oven to 200°C/400°F/Gas Mark 6. Grease or line a deep 12-hole muffin tray with deep paper cases.

2 Finely grate the zest from the lemon into a bowl, then sift in the flour and baking powder and stir in the sugar. In another bowl, beat the eggs with the milk and vanilla extract.

3 Make a well in the centre and pour in the egg mixture and the cooled melted butter. Stir together with a fork until just combined and then gently fold in the blackcurrants.

4 Spoon into the muffin tray and bake for 20 minutes, or until firm and golden. Leave in the tins for 4 minutes, then turn out onto a wire rack to finish cooling. Serve warm or cold. Best eaten on the day of baking.

Ingredients   MAKES 2

1 lemon
275 g/10 oz plain flour
1 tbsp baking powder
125 g/4 oz caster sugar
2 medium eggs
275 ml/9 fl oz milk
$^1/_2$ tsp vanilla extract
75 g/3 oz butter, melted and cooled
150 g/5 oz fresh or frozen
    blackcurrants, trimmed

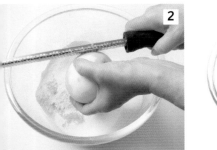

Chocolate Pecan Traybake

1 Preheat the oven to 180°C/350°F/Gas Mark 4, 10 minutes before baking. Lightly oil and line a 28 x 18 x 2.5 cm/11 x 7 x 1 inch cake tin with nonstick baking parchment. Beat the butter and sugar together until light and fluffy. Sift in the flours and cocoa powder and mix together to form a soft dough.

2 Press the mixture evenly over the base of the prepared tin. Prick all over with a fork, then bake on the shelf above the centre of the preheated oven for 15 minutes.

3 Put the butter, sugar, golden syrup, milk and vanilla extract in a small saucepan and heat gently until melted. Remove from the heat and leave to cool for a few minutes, then stir in the eggs and pour over the base. Sprinkle with the nuts.

4 Bake in the preheated oven for 25 minutes, or until dark golden brown, but still slightly soft. Leave to cool in the tin. When cool, carefully remove from the tin, then cut into 12 squares and serve. Store in an airtight container.

Ingredients   MAKES 2

175 g/6 oz butter
75 g/3 oz icing sugar, sifted
175 g/6 oz plain flour
25 g/1 oz self-raising flour
25 g/1 oz cocoa powder

For the pecan topping:
75 g/3 oz butter
50 g/2 oz light muscovado sugar
2 tbsp golden syrup
2 tbsp milk
1 tsp vanilla extract
2 medium eggs, lightly beaten
125 g/4 oz pecan halves

Tasty Tip
Pecans are perfect in this recipe, but if they are unavailable, substitute walnut halves instead.

Sauternes & Olive Oil Cake

1 Preheat the oven to 140°C/275°F/Gas Mark 1. Oil and line a 25.5 cm/10 inch springform tin. Sift the flour onto a large sheet of greaseproof paper and reserve. Using a freestanding electric mixer, if possible, whisk the eggs and sugar together until pale and stiff. Add the lemon and orange zest.

2 Turn the speed to low and pour the flour from the paper in a slow steady stream onto the eggs and sugar mixture. Immediately add the wine and olive oil and switch the machine off as the olive oil should not be incorporated completely.

3 Using a rubber spatula, fold the mixture very gently three or four times so that the ingredients are just incorporated. Pour the mixture immediately into the prepared tin and bake in the preheated oven for 20–25 minutes, without opening the door for at least 15 minutes. Test if cooked by pressing the top lightly with a clean finger – if it springs back, remove from the oven, if not, bake for a little longer.

4 Leave the cake to cool in the tin on a wire rack. Remove the cake from the tin when cool enough to handle.

5 Meanwhile, skin the peaches and cut into segments. Toss with the brown sugar and lemon juice and reserve. When the cake is cold, dust generously with icing sugar, cut into wedges and serve with the peaches.

Ingredients   CUTS INTO
8–10 SLICES

125 g/4 oz plain flour
4 medium eggs
125 g/4 oz caster sugar
grated zest of $^1/_2$ lemon
grated zest of $^1/_2$ orange
2 tbsp Sauternes or other sweet
    dessert wine
3 tbsp very best quality extra virgin
    olive oil
4 ripe peaches
1–2 tsp soft brown sugar, or to taste
1 tbsp lemon juice
icing sugar, for dusting

Helpful Hint

Be careful in step 3 when folding the mixture together not to overmix or the finished cake will be very heavy.

Fruity Buttermilk Muffins

1 Preheat the oven to 200°C/400°F/Gas Mark 6. Line a deep 12-hole muffin tray with deep paper cases. Roughly chop the prunes and set aside.

2 Sift the flours, spice and bicarbonate of soda into a bowl. In another bowl, beat the egg with the marmalade, milk, buttermilk and oil and pour into the dry ingredients.

3 Stir with a fork until just combined, then fold in the apple and chopped prunes. Spoon into the cases and bake for about 20 minutes until golden, risen and firm to the touch.

4 Leave in the tins for 4 minutes, then turn out onto a wire rack to finish cooling. Serve warm or cold and eat on the day of baking.

Ingredients   MAKES 2

125 g/4 oz ready-to-eat
    pitted prunes
175 g/6 oz self-raising flour
50 g/2 oz wholemeal self-raising
    flour
1 tsp mixed ground spice
$\frac{1}{2}$ tsp bicarbonate of soda
1 medium egg
2 tbsp fine-cut orange
    shred marmalade
125 ml/4 fl oz milk
50 ml/2 fl oz buttermilk
5 tbsp sunflower oil
125 g/4 oz eating apple, peeled,
    cored and diced

Chocolate Brazil & Polenta Squares

1 Preheat the oven to 180°C/350°F/Gas Mark 4, 10 minutes before baking. Oil and line a deep 18 cm/7 inch square tin with nonstick baking parchment. Finely chop 50 g/2 oz of the Brazil nuts and reserve. Roughly chop the remainder. Cream the butter and sugar together until light and fluffy. Gradually add the eggs, beating well after each addition.

2 Sift the flour, cocoa powder, cinnamon, baking powder and salt into the creamed mixture and gently fold in using a large metal spoon or spatula. Add the milk, polenta and the roughly chopped Brazil nuts. Fold into the mixture.

3 Turn the mixture into the prepared tin, levelling the surface with the back of the spoon. Sprinkle the reserved finely chopped Brazil nuts over the top. Bake the cake on the centre shelf of the preheated oven for 45–50 minutes until well risen and lightly browned and when a clean skewer inserted into the centre of the cake for a few seconds comes out clean.

4 Leave the cake in the tin for 10 minutes to cool slightly, then turn out onto a wire rack and leave to cool completely. Cut the cake into nine equal squares and serve. Store in an airtight container.

Ingredients

MAKES 9 SQUARES

150 g/5 oz shelled Brazil nuts
150 g/5 oz butter, softened
150 g/5 oz soft light brown sugar
2 medium eggs, lightly beaten
75 g/3 oz plain flour
25 g/1 oz cocoa powder
$1/4$ tsp ground cinnamon
1 tsp baking powder
pinch salt
5 tbsp milk
65 g/$2^1/_2$ oz instant polenta

Tasty Tip

Check the cake after 35 minutes of cooking; if the nuts are starting to brown too much, loosely cover with foil and continue cooking.

Date, Orange & Walnut Muffins

1 Preheat the oven to 200°C/400°F/Gas Mark 6. Line a deep 12-hole muffin tray with deep paper cases.

2 Sift the flour and baking powder into a bowl and make a well in the centre.

3 Add all the remaining ingredients and beat together until just combined. Spoon the batter into the paper cases and bake for about 16–18 minutes until well risen and firm to the touch.

4 Serve warm or cold and eat the muffins on the day of baking.

Ingredients   MAKES 2

275 g/10 oz plain flour
1 tbsp baking powder
125 g/4 oz golden caster sugar
175 g/6 oz stoned dates, chopped
50 g/2 oz walnuts, chopped
1 medium egg
200 ml/7 fl oz milk
finely grated zest and juice
   of 1 orange
6 tbsp sunflower oil

Chocolate Orange Fudge Cake

1 Preheat the oven to 180°C/350°F/Gas Mark 4, 10 minutes before baking. Lightly oil and line two 23 cm/9 inch round cake tins with nonstick baking parchment. Blend the cocoa powder and 50 ml/2 fl oz boiling water until smooth. Stir in the orange zest and reserve. Sift together the flour, baking powder, bicarbonate of soda and salt, then reserve. Cream together the sugar and softened butter and beat in the eggs, one at a time, then the cocoa mixture and vanilla extract. Finally, stir in the flour mixture and the sour cream in alternate spoonfuls.

2 Divide the mixture between the prepared tins and bake in the preheated oven for 35 minutes, or until the edges of the cake pull away from the tin and the tops spring back when lightly pressed. Cool in the tins for 10 minutes, then turn out onto wire racks to cool.

3 Gently heat together the butter and milk with the pared orange rind. Simmer for 10 minutes, stirring occasionally. Remove from the heat and discard the orange rind.

4 Pour the warm orange and milk mixture into a large bowl and stir in the cocoa powder. Gradually beat in the sifted icing sugar and beat until the icing is smooth and spreadable. Place one cake onto a large serving plate. Top with about one quarter of the icing, place the second cake on top, then cover the cake completely with the remaining icing. Serve.

Ingredients

CUTS INTO 8–10 SLICES

65 g/2¹/₂ oz cocoa powder
grated zest of 1 orange
350 g/12 oz self–raising flour
2 tsp baking powder
1 tsp bicarbonate of soda
¹/₂ tsp salt
225 g/8 oz light soft brown sugar
175 g/6 oz butter, softened
3 medium eggs
1 tsp vanilla extract
250 ml/9 fl oz sour cream
6 tbsp butter
6 tbsp milk
thinly pared rind of 1 orange
6 tbsp cocoa powder
250 g/9 oz icing sugar, sifted

Helpful Hint

This cake keeps exceptionally well in an airtight container for up to 5 days

Streusel-topped Banana Muffins

1 Preheat the oven to 200°C/400°F/Gas Mark 6. Line a deep muffin tray with six deep paper cases. Make the topping first by rubbing the butter into the flour until it resembles fine crumbs. Stir in the sugar and cinnamon and set aside.

2 To make the muffins, sift the flours into a bowl, then make a well in the centre. Mash the bananas with a fork and add them to the bowl.

3 In another bowl, beat the egg, oil and milk together and then add them to the bowl. Mix together until evenly blended, then spoon into the muffin cases, filling them two-thirds full.

4 Sprinkle the streusel topping over each muffin and bake for about 25 minutes until golden and a skewer inserted into the centre comes out clean. Eat fresh on the day of baking.

Ingredients   MAKES 6

To decorate:
25 g/1 oz self-raising flour
15 g/^{1}/$_2$ oz butter
40 g/1^1/$_2$ oz demerara sugar
^{1}/$_2$ tsp ground cinnamon

To make the muffins:
125 g/4 oz self-raising wholemeal
   flour
25 g/1 oz plain flour
2 medium, ripe bananas,
   about 175 g/6 oz
1 large egg
50 ml/2 fl oz sunflower oil
50 ml/2 fl oz milk

Chocolate Walnut Squares

1 Preheat the oven to 170˚C/325˚F/Gas Mark 3, 10 minutes before baking. Oil and line a 28 x 18 x 5 cm/11 x 7 x 2 inch cake tin with nonstick baking parchment. Place the butter, chocolate, sugar, vanilla extract and 225 ml/8 fl oz cold water in a heavy-based saucepan. Heat gently, stirring occasionally, until the chocolate and butter have melted, but do not allow to boil.

2 Sift the flours and cocoa powder into a large bowl and make a well in the centre. Add the mayonnaise and about one third of the chocolate mixture and beat until smooth. Gradually beat in the remaining chocolate mixture. Pour into the tin and bake on the centre shelf of the oven for 1 hour, or until slightly risen and firm to the touch. Place the tin on a wire rack and leave to cool. Remove the cake and peel off the baking parchment.

3 For the chocolate glaze, place the chocolate and butter in a small saucepan with 1 tablespoon water and heat very gently, stirring occasionally, until melted and smooth. Leave to cool until the chocolate has thickened, then spread evenly over the cake. Chill the cake in the refrigerator for about 5 minutes, then mark into 24 squares.

4 Lightly dust the walnut halves with a little icing sugar and place one on the top of each square. Cut into pieces and store in an airtight container until ready to serve.

Ingredients   MAKES 24

125 g/4 oz butter
150 g/5 oz dark chocolate, broken
   into squares
450 g/1 lb caster sugar
$^{1}/_{2}$ tsp vanilla extract
200 g/7 oz plain flour
75 g/3 oz self-raising flour
50 g/2 oz cocoa powder
225 g/8 oz mayonnaise, at
   room temperature

For the chocolate glaze:
125 g/4 oz dark chocolate, broken
   into squares
40 g/1$^{1}/_{2}$ oz unsalted butter
24 walnut halves
1 tbsp icing sugar, for dusting

Tasty Tip
Mayonnaise is used in this recipe instead of eggs. Make sure you use a plain and not flavoured mayonnaise.

Pistachio Muffins

1   Preheat the oven to 200°C/400°F/Gas Mark 6. Line a deep 12-hole muffin tray with 10 deep paper cases. Roughly chop the 50 g/2 oz pistachio nuts.

2   Sift the flour into a bowl and add the butter, sugar and eggs. Beat for about 2 minutes, then fold in the syrup and chopped nuts.

3   Spoon the mixture into the paper cases and bake for about 20 minutes until well risen and springy in the centre. Remove to a wire rack to cool.

4   To decorate the cakes, sift the icing sugar into a bowl, then add the butter, lemon juice and 1 tablespoon hot water. Beat until light and fluffy, then swirl onto each muffin with a small palette knife. Place the chopped pistachio nuts in a small shallow bowl. Dip the top of each muffin into the nuts to make an attractive topping. Keep for 4 days in an airtight container in a cool place.

Ingredients   MAKES 10

50 g/2 oz pistachio nuts
125 g/4 oz self-raising flour
125 g/4 oz butter, softened
125 g/4 oz golden caster sugar
2 medium eggs, beaten
1 tbsp maple syrup or golden syrup

To decorate:
225 g/8 oz golden icing sugar
125 g/4 oz unsalted butter, softened
2 tsp lemon juice
25 g/1 oz pistachio nuts, chopped

Crunchy-topped Citrus Chocolate Slices

1 Preheat the oven to 170 C/325 F/Gas Mark 3, 10 minutes before baking. Oil and line a 28 x 18 x 2.5 cm/11 x 7 x 1 inch cake tin with nonstick baking parchment. Place the butter, sugar and orange zest into a large bowl and cream together until light and fluffy. Gradually add the eggs, beating after each addition, then beat in the ground almonds.

2 Sift the flour and baking powder into the creamed mixture. Add the grated chocolate and milk, then gently fold in using a metal spoon. Spoon the mixture into the prepared tin.

3 Bake on the centre shelf of the preheated oven for 35–40 minutes until well risen and firm to the touch. Leave in the tin for a few minutes to cool slightly. Turn out onto a wire rack and remove the baking parchment.

4 Meanwhile, to make the crunchy topping, place the sugar with the lime and orange juices into a small jug and stir together. Drizzle the sugar mixture over the hot cake, ensuring the whole surface is covered. Leave until completely cold, then cut into 12 slices and serve.

Ingredients

CUTS INTO
12 SLICES

175 g/6 oz butter
175 g/6 oz soft light brown sugar
finely grated zest of 1 orange
3 medium eggs, lightly beaten
1 tbsp ground almonds
175 g/6 oz self–raising flour
$1/4$ tsp baking powder
125 g/4 oz dark chocolate,
   coarsely grated
2 tsp milk

For the crunchy topping:
125 g/4 oz granulated sugar
juice of 2 limes
juice of 1 orange

Helpful Hint
It is important that the cake is still hot from the oven when the citrus topping is added, otherwise it will simply sit on the cake.

Peaches & Cream Muffins

1 Preheat the oven to 190°C/375°F/Gas Mark 5. Line a deep 12-hole muffin tray with 10 paper cases. Drain the peaches and chop 125 g/4 oz into small chunks.

2 Sift the flours and cinnamon into a bowl, adding any bran from the sieve, then add the butter, sugar and eggs. Beat for about 2 minutes, then fold in the golden syrup and chopped peaches.

3 Spoon the mixture into the paper cases and bake for about 20 minutes until well risen and springy in the centre. Remove to a wire rack to cool.

4 Place 50 g/2 oz sliced peaches in a blender or food processor with the lemon juice and icing sugar to make a purée (the rest of the can's weight is syrup). Whip the cream until it forms soft peaks and then fold in half the purée. Place a large spoonful of cream on top of each muffin, then swirl in a little extra purée. Refrigerate until needed and eat within 24 hours.

Ingredients MAKES 10

225 g/8 oz can peach slices or
    halves in syrup
125 g/4 oz self-raising flour
50 g/2 oz wholemeal self-raising flour
$^1/_2$ tsp cinnamon
175 g/6 oz butter, softened
175 g/6 oz golden caster sugar
3 medium eggs, beaten
1 tbsp golden syrup

To decorate:

2 tsp lemon juice
2 tbsp icing sugar
150 ml/$^1/_4$ pint whipping cream

Marbled Chocolate Traybake

1 Preheat the oven to 180 C/350 F/Gas Mark 4, 10 minutes before baking. Oil and line a 28 x 18 x 2.5 cm/11 x 7 x 1 inch cake tin with nonstick baking parchment. Cream the butter, sugar and vanilla extract until light and fluffy. Gradually add the eggs, beating well after each addition. Sift in the flour and baking powder and fold in with the milk.

2 Spoon half the mixture into the prepared tin, spacing the spoonfuls apart and leaving gaps in between. Blend the cocoa powder to a smooth paste with 2 tablespoons warm water. Stir this into the remaining cake mixture. Drop small spoonfuls between the vanilla cake mixture to fill in all the gaps. Use a knife to swirl the mixtures together a little.

3 Bake on the centre shelf of the preheated oven for 35 minutes, or until well risen and firm to the touch. Leave in the tin for 5 minutes to cool, then turn out onto a wire rack and leave to cool. Remove the baking parchment.

4 For the icing, place the plain and white chocolate in separate heatproof bowls and melt each over a saucepan of almost boiling water. Spoon into separate nonstick baking parchment piping bags, snip off the tips and drizzle over the top. Leave to set before cutting into squares.

Ingredients

MAKES 8 SQUARES

175 g/6 oz butter
175 g/6 oz caster sugar
1 tsp vanilla extract
3 medium eggs, lightly beaten
200 g/7 oz self-raising flour
$\frac{1}{2}$ tsp baking powder
1 tbsp milk
$1\frac{1}{2}$ tbsp cocoa powder

For the chocolate icing:

75 g/3 oz dark chocolate, broken
    into pieces
75 g/3 oz white chocolate, broken
    into pieces

Tasty Tip

To marble the topping, spread the dark chocolate evenly over the top of the cake. Put the white chocolate in a small piping bag and drizzle over the dark chocolate in random circles. Use a cocktail stick or skewer to drag the two chocolates together.

2

2

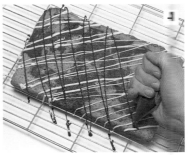

4

Light White Chocolate & Walnut Blondies

1 Preheat the oven to 190°C/375°F/Gas Mark 5, 10 minutes before baking. Oil and line a 28 x 18 x 2.5 cm/11 x 7 x 1 inch cake tin with nonstick baking parchment. Place the butter and demerara sugar into a heavy-based saucepan and heat gently until the butter has melted and the sugar has started to dissolve. Remove from the heat and leave to cool.

2 Place the eggs, vanilla extract and milk in a large bowl and beat together. Stir in the butter and sugar mixture, then sift in the 125 g/4 oz of flour, the baking powder and salt. Gently stir the mixture twice.

3 Toss the walnuts and chocolate drops in the remaining 1 tablespoon of flour to coat. Add to the bowl and stir the ingredients together gently.

4 Spoon the mixture into the prepared tin and bake on the centre shelf of the preheated oven for 35 minutes, or until the top is firm and slightly crusty. Place the tin on a wire rack and leave to cool.

5 When completely cold, remove the cake from the tin and lightly dust the top with icing sugar. Cut into 16 blondies using a sharp knife, and serve.

Ingredients
SERVES 8

75 g/3 oz unsalted butter
200 g/7 oz demerara sugar
2 large eggs, lightly beaten
1 tsp vanilla extract
2 tbsp milk
125 g/4 oz plain flour, plus 1 tbsp
1 tsp baking powder
pinch salt
75 g/3 oz walnuts, roughly chopped
125 g/4 oz white chocolate drops
1 tbsp icing sugar, for dusting

Tasty Tip

For a chocolate topping, mix together about 50 g/2 oz each of white, milk and plain chocolate chips. Sprinkle over the hot blondies as soon as they are removed from the oven. Leave the cake to cool. Cut into squares and serve from the tin.

Rhubarb & Custard Muffins

1 Preheat the oven to 180°C/350°F/Gas Mark 4. Oil or line a 12-hole deep muffin tray with deep muffin cases. Chop the rhubarb into pieces 1 cm/^{1}/$_2$ inch long.

2 Sift the custard powder, flour and baking powder into a bowl and stir in the sugar. In another bowl, beat the milk, eggs and vanilla extract together. Make a well in the centre of the dry ingredients and pour in the milk mixture.

3 Add the melted butter and beat together with a fork until just combined, then fold in the chopped rhubarb. Spoon the mixture into the cases and bake for 15–20 minutes until golden, risen and firm in the centre.

4 Leave in the tray to firm up for 5 minutes, then turn out onto a wire rack to cool. Serve warm, dusted with golden caster sugar. Eat on the day of baking.

Ingredients   MAKES 12

225 g/8 oz pink rhubarb
25 g/1 oz vanilla custard powder
175 g/6 oz plain flour
2 tsp baking powder
125 g/4 oz golden caster sugar
100 ml/3^1/$_2$ fl oz milk
2 medium eggs, beaten
^{1}/$_2$ tsp vanilla extract
125 g/4 oz butter, melted and cooled
golden caster sugar, for dusting

Cappuccino Cakes

1 Preheat the oven to 190°C/375°F/Gas Mark 5, 10 minutes before baking. Place six large paper muffin cases into a muffin tray or alternatively place onto a baking sheet.

2 Cream the butter or margarine and sugar together until light and fluffy. Break the eggs into a small bowl and beat lightly with a fork.

3 Using a wooden spoon, beat the eggs into the butter and sugar mixture a little at a time, until they are all incorporated. If the mixture looks curdled, beat in a spoonful of the flour to return the mixture to a smooth consistency. Finally, beat in the black coffee.

4 Sift the flour into the mixture, then, with a metal spoon or rubber spatula gently fold in the flour. Place spoonfuls of the mixture into the muffin cases. Bake in the preheated oven for 20–25 minutes until risen and springy to the touch. Cool on a wire rack.

5 In a small bowl, beat together the mascarpone cheese, icing sugar and vanilla extract. When the cakes are cold, spoon the vanilla mascarpone onto the top of each one. Dust with cocoa powder and serve. Eat within 24 hours and store in the refrigerator.

Ingredients   MAKES 6

125 g/4 oz butter or margarine
125 g/4 oz caster sugar
2 medium eggs
1 tbsp strong black coffee
150 g/5 oz self-raising flour
125 g/4 oz mascarpone cheese
1 tbsp icing sugar, sifted
1 tsp vanilla extract
cocoa powder, sifted, for dusting

Tasty Tip

The combination of coffee with the vanilla-flavoured mascarpone is heavenly! Make sure, however, that you use a good-quality coffee in this recipe. Colombian coffee is generally good and at its best possesses a smooth rounded flavour

Ginger & Apricot Mini Muffins

1 Preheat the oven to 200°C/400°F/Gas Mark 6. Line one or two mini-muffin trays with 18 mini paper cases. Finely chop the apricots and set aside.

2 Sift the flours, baking powder and cinnamon into a bowl, adding any bran from the sieve, then stir in the sugar. In another bowl, beat the egg and milk together and then pour into the dry ingredients.

3 Add the melted butter, apricots, ginger and half the almonds and mix quickly with a fork until just combined.

4 Spoon the mixture into the cases. Scatter the other half of the almonds and the sugar crystals over the top. Bake for 15–20 minutes until risen and golden. Turn out onto a wire rack to cool and eat fresh on the day of baking.

Ingredients   MAKES 18

125 g/4 oz canned apricots, drained
75 g/3 oz plain flour
75 g/3 oz wholemeal flour
2 tsp baking powder
$1/2$ tsp ground cinnamon
50 g/2 oz soft light brown sugar
1 medium egg
135 ml/$4^{1}/_{2}$ fl oz milk
75 g/3 oz butter, melted
50 g/2 oz glacé ginger, chopped
50 g/2 oz almonds, chopped
sparkly sugar pieces, to decorate

Maple, Pecan & Lemon Loaf

1 Preheat the oven to 170°C/325°F/Gas Mark 3, 10 minutes before baking. Lightly oil and line the base of a 900 g/ 2 lb loaf tin with nonstick baking parchment.

2 Sift the flour and baking powder into a large bowl. Rub in the butter until the mixture resembles fine breadcrumbs. Stir in the caster sugar and pecan nuts.

3 Beat the eggs together with the milk and lemon zest. Stir in the maple syrup. Add to the dry ingredients and gently stir in until mixed thoroughly to make a soft dropping consistency.

4 Spoon the mixture into the prepared tin and level the top with the back of a spoon. Bake on the middle shelf of the preheated oven for 50–60 minutes until the loaf is well risen and lightly browned. If a skewer inserted into the centre comes out clean, then the loaf is ready.

5 Leave the loaf in the tin for about 10 minutes, then turn out and leave to cool on a wire rack. Carefully remove the lining paper.

6 Sift the icing sugar into a small bowl and stir in the lemon juice to make a smooth icing. Drizzle the icing over the top of the loaf, then scatter with the chopped pecans. Leave to set, thickly slice and serve.

Ingredients
CUTS INTO 12 SLICES

350 g/12 oz plain flour
1 tsp baking powder
175 g/6 oz butter, cubed
75 g/3 oz caster sugar
125 g/4 oz pecan nuts,
 roughly chopped
3 medium eggs
1 tbsp milk
finely grated zest of 1 lemon
5 tbsp maple syrup

For the icing:
75 g/3 oz icing sugar
1 tbsp lemon juice
25 g/1 oz pecans, roughly
 chopped

Helpful Hint
If the top of the cake starts to brown too much during cooking, loosely cover with a piece of foil.

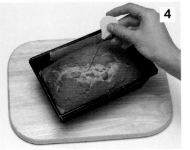

Marmalade Loaf Cake

1 Preheat the oven to 180°C/350°F/Gas Mark 4. Grease and line a 1 kg/2 lb loaf tin with a long thin strip of nonstick baking parchment.

2 Place the sugar and butter in a bowl and whisk until light and fluffy. Add the beaten eggs a little at a time, adding 1 teaspoon flour with each addition.

3 Add the remaining flour to the bowl with the orange zest, 2 tablespoons orange juice and the marmalade. Using a large metal spoon, fold the mixture together using a figure-of-eight movement until all the flour is incorporated. Spoon the mixture into the tin and smooth level.

4 Bake for about 40 minutes until firm in the centre and a skewer inserted into the centre comes out clean. Cool in the tin for 5 minutes, then turn out to cool on a wire rack.

5 To make the topping, peel thin strips of zest away from the orange and set aside. Squeeze the juice from the orange. Sift the icing sugar into a bowl and mix with 1 tablespoon of the orange juice until a thin smooth consistency forms. Drizzle over the top of the cake, letting it run down the sides. Scatter over the orange zest and leave to set for 1 hour.

Ingredients   CUTS INTO
8–10 SLICES

175 g/6 oz natural golden caster sugar
175 g/6 oz butter, softened
3 medium eggs, beaten
175 g/6 oz self-raising flour
finely grated zest and juice of
  1 orange
100 g/3$^1/_2$ oz orange marmalade

For the topping:
zest and juice of 1 orange
125 g/4 oz icing sugar

Chocolate Chiffon Cake

1 Preheat the oven to 170°C/325°F/Gas Mark 3, 10 minutes before baking. Lightly oil and line a 23 cm/9 inch round cake tin. Lightly oil a baking sheet. Blend the cocoa powder with 175 ml/6 fl oz boiling water and leave to cool. Place the flour and 350 g/12 oz of the caster sugar in a large bowl. Add the cocoa mixture, egg yolks, oil and vanilla extract. Whisk until smooth and lighter in colour. Whisk the egg whites in a clean, grease-free bowl until soft peaks form, then fold into the cocoa mixture. Pour into the tin and bake for 1 hour, or until firm. Leave for 5 minutes; turn out onto a wire rack to cool.

2 For the icing, cream together 125 g/4 oz of the butter with the icing sugar, cocoa powder and brandy until smooth, then reserve. Melt the remaining butter and blend with 150 g/5 oz of the melted dark chocolate. Stir until smooth and then leave until thickened. Place the remaining caster sugar into a heavy-based saucepan over a low heat and heat until the sugar has melted and is a deep golden brown. Add the walnuts and the remaining melted chocolate to the melted sugar and pour onto the baking sheet. Leave until cold and brittle, then chop finely. Reserve.

3 Split the cake into 3 layers. Place 1 layer onto a plate and spread with half of the brandy butter icing. Top with a second cake layer, spread with the remaining brandy butter icing; arrange the third cake layer on top. Cover the cake with the thickened chocolate glaze. Sprinkle with the walnut praline and serve.

Ingredients

CUTS INTO 10–12 SLICES

50 g/2 oz cocoa powder
300 g/11 oz self-raising flour
550 g/1 lb 3 oz caster sugar
7 medium eggs, separated
125 ml/4 fl oz vegetable oil
1 tsp vanilla extract
75 g/3 oz walnuts
200 g/7 oz dark chocolate, melted

For the icing:

175 g/6 oz butter
275 g/10 oz icing sugar, sifted
2 tbsp cocoa powder, sifted
2 tbsp brandy

Helpful Hint

Do not overmix the mixture in step 1 or the cake will be heavy instead of very light and spongy.

Apricot & Almond Slice

1 Preheat the oven to 180°C/350°F/Gas Mark 4. Oil a 20.5 cm/ 8 inch square tin and line with nonstick baking parchment.

2 Sprinkle the sugar and the flaked almonds over the paper, then arrange the apricot halves cut-side down on top.

3 Cream the butter and sugar together in a large bowl until light and fluffy.

4 Gradually beat the eggs into the butter mixture, adding a spoonful of flour after each addition of egg.

5 When all the eggs have been added, stir in the remaining flour and ground almonds and mix thoroughly.

6 Add the almond extract and the apricots and stir well.

7 Spoon the mixture into the prepared tin, taking care not to dislodge the apricot halves. Bake in the preheated oven for 1 hour, or until golden and firm to the touch.

8 Remove from the oven and allow to cool slightly for 15–20 minutes. Turn out carefully, discard the lining paper and transfer to a serving dish. Pour the honey over the top of the cake, sprinkle on the toasted almonds and serve.

Ingredients
CUTS INTO 10 SLICES

2 tbsp demerara sugar
25 g/1 oz flaked almonds
400 g can apricot halves, drained
225 g/8 oz butter
225 g/8 oz caster sugar
4 medium eggs
200 g/7 oz self-raising flour
25 g/1 oz ground almonds
$1/_2$ tsp almond extract
50 g/2 oz ready-to-eat dried
    apricots, chopped
3 tbsp clear honey
3 tbsp roughly chopped
    almonds, toasted

Helpful Hint
This cake should keep for about 3–5 days if stored correctly. Allow to cool completely then remove from the tin and discard the lining paper. Store in an airtight container lined with greaseproof paper or baking parchment and keep in a cool place.

Special Everyday Cakes

Who says you need a special occasion to make a special cake? The recipes in this section are a little simpler, but the delicious Lemon Drizzle Cake and the Victoria Sponge with Mango and Mascarpone are luxurious enough to have you celebrating even on the most regular of days!

Luxury Carrot Cake

1 Preheat the oven to 180°C/350°F/Gas Mark 4, 10 minutes before baking. Lightly oil a 33 x 23 cm/13 x 9 inch baking tin. Line the base with nonstick baking parchment, oil and dust with flour.

2 Sift the first six ingredients into a large bowl and stir in the sugars to blend. Make a well in the centre.

3 Beat the eggs, oil and vanilla extract together and pour into the well. Using an electric whisk, gradually beat, drawing in the flour mixture from the sides until a smooth batter forms. Stir in the carrots, crushed pineapple and chopped nuts until blended.

4 Pour into the prepared tin and smooth the surface evenly. Bake in the preheated oven for 50 minutes, or until firm and a skewer inserted into the centre comes out clean. Remove from the oven and leave to cool before removing from the tin and discarding the lining paper.

5 For the frosting, beat the cream cheese, butter and vanilla extract together until smooth, then gradually beat in the icing sugar until the frosting is smooth. Add a little milk, if necessary. Spread the frosting over the top. Refrigerate for about 1 hour to set the frosting, then cut into squares and serve.

Ingredients   12 SLICES

275 g/10 oz plain flour
2 tsp baking powder
1 tsp bicarbonate of soda
1 tsp salt
2 tsp ground cinnamon
1 tsp ground ginger
200 g/7 oz soft dark brown sugar
100 g/3^1/$_2$ oz caster sugar
4 large eggs, beaten
250 ml/9 fl oz sunflower oil
1 tbsp vanilla extract
4 carrots, peeled and shredded
    (about 450 g/1 lb)
400 g/14 oz can crushed pineapple,
    well drained
125 g/4 oz pecans or walnuts,
    toasted and chopped

For the frosting:

175 g/6 oz cream cheese, softened
50 g/2 oz butter, softened
1 tsp vanilla extract
225 g/8 oz icing sugar, sifted
1–2 tbsp milk, if needed

Gingerbread

1 Preheat the oven to 150°C/300°F/Gas Mark 2, 10 minutes before baking. Lightly oil and line the base of a 20.5 cm/ 8 inch deep round cake tin with greaseproof paper or baking parchment.

2 In a saucepan, gently heat the butter or margarine, black treacle and sugar, stirring occasionally until the butter melts. Leave to cool slightly.

3 Sift the flour and ground ginger into a large bowl. Make a well in the centre, then pour in the treacle mixture. Reserve 1 tablespoon of the milk, then pour the rest into the treacle mixture. Stir together lightly until mixed.

4 Beat the eggs together, then stir into the mixture. Dissolve the bicarbonate of soda in the remaining 1 tablespoon of the warmed milk and add to the mixture.

5 Beat the mixture until well mixed and free of lumps. Pour into the prepared tin and bake in the preheated oven for 1 hour, or until well risen and a skewer inserted into the centre comes out clean.

6 Cool in the tin, then remove. Slice the stem ginger into thin slivers and sprinkle over the cake. Drizzle with the syrup and serve.

Ingredients

CUTS INTO 8 SLICES

175 g/6 oz butter or margarine
225 g/8 oz black treacle
50 g/2 oz dark muscovado sugar
350 g/12 oz plain flour
2 tsp ground ginger
150 ml/¼ pint milk, warmed
2 medium eggs
1 tsp bicarbonate of soda
1 piece stem ginger in syrup
1 tbsp stem ginger syrup

Food Fact

There are many different types of gingerbread, ranging in colour from a deep rich dark brown to a light golden. This is due to the type of treacle and the amount of bicarbonate of soda used. One well-known gingerbread from Yorkshire is Parkin, which uses both golden syrup and black treacle

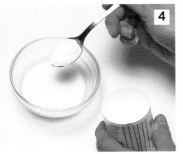

Toffee Apple Cake

1 Preheat the oven to 180°C/350°F/Gas Mark 4, 10 minutes before baking. Lightly oil and line the bases of two 20.5 cm/8 inch sandwich tins with greaseproof paper or baking parchment.

2 Thinly slice the apples and toss in the brown sugar until well coated. Arrange them over the base of the prepared tins and reserve.

3 Cream together the butter or margarine and caster sugar until light and fluffy.

4 Beat the eggs together in a small bowl and gradually beat them into the creamed mixture, beating well after each addition. Sift the flour into the mixture and, using a metal spoon or rubber spatula, fold in.

5 Divide the mixture between the two cake tins and level the surface. Bake in the preheated oven for 25–30 minutes until golden and well risen. Leave in the tins to cool.

6 Lightly whip the cream with 1 tablespoon of the icing sugar and vanilla extract.

7 Sandwich the cakes together with the cream. Mix the remaining icing sugar and ground cinnamon together, sprinkle over the top of the cake and serve.

Ingredients
CUTS INTO 8 SLICES

2 small eating apples, peeled
4 tbsp soft dark brown sugar
175 g/6 oz butter or margarine
175 g/6 oz caster sugar
3 medium eggs
175 g/6 oz self-raising flour
150 ml/$^1/_4$ pint double cream
2 tbsp icing sugar
$^1/_2$ tsp vanilla extract
$^1/_2$ tsp ground cinnamon

Tasty Tip
The dark brown sugar used in this recipe could be replaced with a dark muscovado sugar to give a delicious rich toffee flavour to the apples. When baked, the sugar will melt slightly into a caramel consistency.

Lemon Drizzle Cake

1   Preheat the oven to 180°C/350°F/Gas Mark 4, 10 minutes before baking. Lightly oil and line the base of an 18 cm/7 inch square cake tin with baking parchment.

2   In a large bowl, cream the butter or margarine and sugar together until soft and fluffy. Beat the eggs, then gradually add a little of the egg to the creamed mixture, adding 1 tablespoon of the flour after each addition.

3   Finely grate the zest from one of the lemons and stir into the creamed mixture, beating well until smooth. Squeeze the juice from the lemon, strain, then stir into the mixture.

4   Spoon into the tin, level the surface and bake in the oven for 25–30 minutes. Using a zester, remove the peel from the last lemon and mix with 25 g/1 oz of the granulated sugar. Reserve.

5   Squeeze the juice into a small saucepan. Add the rest of the granulated sugar to the lemon juice in the saucepan and heat gently, stirring occasionally. When the sugar has dissolved, simmer gently for 3–4 minutes until syrupy.

6   With a cocktail stick or fine skewer, prick the cake all over. Sprinkle the lemon zest and sugar over the top of the cake, drizzle over the syrup and leave to cool in the tin. Cut the cake into squares and serve.

Ingredients

MAKES 15 SQUARES

125 g/4 oz butter or margarine
175 g/6 oz caster sugar
2 large eggs
175 g/6 oz self-raising flour
2 lemons, preferably unwaxed
50 g/2 oz granulated sugar

Food Fact

This classic cake is a favourite in many kitchens. The buttery sponge is perfectly complemented by the lemon syrup, which soaks into the cake, giving it a gooeyness which is even better the next day!

Chunky Chocolate Muffins

1 Preheat the oven to 200°C/400°F/Gas Mark 6, 15 minutes before baking. Line a muffin tray or deep bun tin with seven paper muffin cases or oil the individual compartments well. Place the plain chocolate in a large heatproof bowl set over a saucepan of simmering water and stir occasionally until melted. Remove the bowl and leave to cool for a few minutes.

2 Stir the sugar and butter into the melted chocolate, then the milk, vanilla extract and egg. Sift in the flour, baking powder and salt together. Add the chopped white chocolate, then, using a metal spoon, fold together quickly, taking care not to overmix.

3 Divide the mixture between the paper cases, piling it up in the centre. Bake on the centre shelf of the preheated oven for 20–25 minutes until well risen and firm to the touch.

4 Lightly dust the tops of the muffins with icing sugar, if using, as soon as they come out of the oven. Leave the muffins in the tin for a few minutes, then transfer to a wire rack. Serve warm or cold.

Ingredients   MAKES 7

50 g/2 oz plain dark chocolate, roughly chopped
50 g/2 oz light muscovado sugar
25 g/1 oz butter, melted
125 ml/4 fl oz milk, heated to room temperature
$\frac{1}{2}$ tsp vanilla extract
1 medium egg, lightly beaten
150 g/5 oz self–raising flour
$\frac{1}{2}$ tsp baking powder
pinch salt
75 g/3 oz white chocolate, chopped
2 tsp icing sugar (optional)

Helpful Hint

If you do not have a large muffin tray or deep bun tin, you can use an ordinary bun tin with cake cases, in which case the quantities given will make 10–12 smaller muffins.

Dundee Cake

1 Preheat the oven to 180°C/350°F/Gas Mark 4. Grease and line the base of an 18 cm/7 inch deep round cake tin with nonstick baking parchment.

2 Place the dried fruit in a bowl and stir in the ground almonds to coat the dried fruit.

3 Finely grate the zest from the lemon into the bowl, then squeeze out 1 tablespoon of juice and add to the same bowl. In another bowl, beat the butter and sugar together until light and fluffy. Whisk in the eggs a little at a time, adding 1 teaspoon of the flour with each addition.

4 Sift in the remaining flour, then add the fruit and almond mixture. Fold together with a large metal spoon until smooth. Spoon the mixture into the tin and make a dip in the centre with the back of a spoon. Arrange the almonds over the top in circles.

5 Bake for 1 hour, then reduce the heat to 150°C/300°F/Gas Mark 2 and bake for a further hour, or until a skewer inserted into the centre comes out clean. Cool in the tin for 5 minutes, then turn out to cool on a wire rack.

Ingredients   SERVES 8– ⊃

400 g/14 oz mixed dried fruit
50 g/2 oz ground almonds
finely grated zest and juice
    of 1 lemon
150 g/5 oz butter, at
    room temperature
150 g/5 oz natural golden caster sugar
3 medium eggs, beaten
125 g/4 oz plain flour
40 g/1½ oz whole blanched almonds

Honey Cake

1 Preheat the oven to 180°C/350°F/Gas Mark 4, 10 minutes before baking. Lightly oil and line the base of an 18 cm/7 inch deep round cake tin with lightly oiled greaseproof or baking paper.

2 In a saucepan, gently heat the butter, sugar and honey until the butter has just melted. Sift the flour, bicarbonate of soda and mixed spice together into a bowl.

3 Beat the egg and the milk until mixed thoroughly.

4 Make a well in the centre of the sifted flour and pour in the melted butter and honey. Using a wooden spoon, beat well, gradually drawing in the flour from the sides of the bowl. When all the flour has been beaten in, add the egg mixture and mix thoroughly. Pour into the tin and sprinkle with the flaked almonds.

5 Bake in the oven for 30–35 minutes, or until well risen and golden brown and a skewer inserted into the centre of the cake comes out clean.

6 Remove from the oven and cool for a few minutes in the tin before turning out and leaving to cool on a wire rack. Drizzle with the remaining tablespoon of honey and serve.

Ingredients
CUTS INTO
6 SLICES

50 g/2 oz butter
25 g/1 oz caster sugar
125 g/4 oz clear honey
175 g/6 oz plain flour
$^1/_2$ tsp bicarbonate of soda
$^1/_2$ tsp mixed spice
1 medium egg
2 tbsp milk
25 g/1 oz flaked almonds
1 tbsp clear honey, for drizzling

Tasty Tip
Serve a slice of this cake with a large spoonful of Greek yogurt on the side. The tart taste of the yogurt complements the sweetness of the honey and spice perfectly – ideal for an afternoon treat.

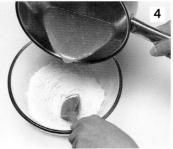

Chestnut Cake

1 Preheat the oven to 150°C/300°F/Gas Mark 2. Oil and line a 23 cm/9 inch springform tin. Beat together the butter and sugar until light and fluffy. Add the chestnut purée and beat. Gradually add the eggs, beating after each addition. Sift in the flour with the baking powder and cloves. Add the fennel seeds and beat. The mixture should drop easily from a wooden spoon when tapped against the side of the bowl. If not, add a little milk.

2 Beat in the raisins and pine nuts. Spoon the mixture into the prepared tin and smooth the top. Transfer to the centre of the preheated oven and bake for 55–60 minutes until a skewer inserted in the centre of the cake comes out clean. Remove from the oven and leave in the tin.

3 Meanwhile, mix together the icing sugar and lemon juice in a small saucepan until smooth. Heat gently until hot, but not boiling. Using a cocktail stick or skewer, poke holes into the cake all over. Pour the hot syrup evenly over the cake and leave to soak into the cake. Decorate with pared strips of lemon and serve.

Ingredients   SERVES 8– 0

175 g/6 oz butter, softened
175 g/6 oz caster sugar
250 g can sweetened chestnut purée
3 medium eggs, lightly beaten
175 g/6 oz plain flour
1 tsp baking powder
pinch ground cloves
1 tsp fennel seeds, crushed
75 g/3 oz raisins
50 g/2 oz pine nuts, toasted
125 g/4 oz icing sugar
5 tbsp lemon juice
pared strips of lemon rind, to decorate

Almond Cake

1 Preheat the oven to 180°C/350°F/Gas Mark 4. Lightly oil and line the base of a 20.5 cm/8 inch deep round cake tin with greaseproof paper or baking parchment.

2 Cream together the butter or margarine and sugar with a wooden spoon until light and fluffy. Beat the eggs and extracts together. Gradually add to the sugar and butter mixture and mix well after each addition.

3 Sift the flour and mix with the ground almonds. Beat into the egg mixture until well mixed and smooth. Pour into the prepared cake tin.

4 Roughly chop the whole almonds and scatter over the cake before baking in the preheated oven.

5 Bake in the preheated oven for 45 minutes, or until golden and risen and a skewer inserted into the centre of the cake comes out clean.

6 Remove from the tin and leave to cool on a wire rack. Melt the chocolate in a small bowl placed over a saucepan of gently simmering water, stirring until smooth and free of lumps.

7 Drizzle the melted chocolate over the cooled cake and serve once the chocolate has set.

Ingredients

8UTS INTO
8 SLICS

225 g/8 oz butter or margarine
225 g/8 oz caster sugar
3 large eggs
1 tsp vanilla extract
1 tsp almond extract
125 g/4 oz self-raising flour
175 g/6 oz ground almonds
50 g/2 oz whole
   almonds, blanched
25 g/1 oz plain dark chocolate

Tasty Tip

Baking with ground almonds helps to keep the cake moist as well as adding a slight nutty flavour to the cake. 1–2 tablespoons orange water can be added with the zest of 1 orange in step 2 if a fragrant citrus flavour is desired, but do omit the vanilla extract.

2

4

7

Blueberry Buttermilk Muffins

1   Preheat the oven to 180°C/350°F/Gas Mark 4. Line a deep muffin tray with six to eight paper cases, depending on the depth of the holes.

2   Sift the flour and baking powder into a bowl, then add the sugar. In another bowl, beat the buttermilk with the egg and vanilla extract, then pour into the dry ingredients. Mix with a fork, then add the cooled melted butter and stir until mixed but still slightly lumpy.

3   Gently fold in the blueberries. Spoon the mixture into the muffin cases, filling each two–thirds full. Bake for about 20 minutes until springy in the centre. Leave in the trays for 5 minutes, then turn out onto a wire rack to finish cooling. Eat warm or cold on the day of baking.

Ingredients

MAKES 6–8

175 g/6 oz plain flour
1 tsp baking powder
175 g/6 oz golden caster sugar
175 ml/6 fl oz buttermilk
1 medium egg
$^1/_2$ tsp vanilla extract
40 g/1$^1/_2$ oz butter, melted
     and cooled
150 g/5 oz fresh blueberries

Apple & Cinnamon Crumble-top Cake

1 Preheat the oven to 180°C/350°F/Gas Mark 4, 10 minutes before baking. Lightly oil and line the base of a 20.5 cm/8 inch deep round cake tin with greaseproof paper or baking parchment.

2 Finely chop the apples and mix with the lemon juice. Reserve while making the cake.

3 For the crumble topping, sift the flour and cinnamon together into a large bowl. Rub the butter or margarine into the flour and cinnamon until the mixture resembles coarse breadcrumbs. Stir the sugar into the breadcrumbs and reserve.

4 For the base, cream the butter or margarine and sugar together until light and fluffy. Gradually beat the eggs into the sugar and butter mixture a little at a time until all the egg has been added.

5 Sift the flour and gently fold in with a metal spoon or rubber spatula.

6 Spoon into the base of the prepared cake tin. Arrange the apple pieces on top, then lightly stir the milk into the crumble mixture.

7 Scatter the crumble mixture over the apples and bake in the preheated oven for 1½ hours. Serve cold with cream or custard.

Ingredients

CUTS INTO
8 SLICES

For the topping:
350 g/12 oz eating apples, peeled
1 tbsp lemon juice
125 g/4 oz self-raising flour
1 tsp ground cinnamon
75 g/3 oz butter or margarine
75 g/3 oz demerara sugar
1 tbsp milk

For the base:
125 g/4 oz butter or margarine
125 g/4 oz caster sugar
2 medium eggs
150 g/5 oz self-raising flour
cream or freshly made custard, to serve

Tasty Tip
For a crunchier-textured topping, stir 50 g/2 oz chopped mixed nuts and seeds into the crumble mixture in step 3.

Fresh Strawberry Sponge Cake

1 Preheat the oven to 190°C/375°F/Gas Mark 5, 10 minutes before baking. Lightly oil and line the bases of two 20.5 cm/ 8 inch round cake tins with greaseproof paper or baking parchment.

2 Using an electric whisk, beat the butter, sugar and vanilla extract until pale and fluffy. Gradually beat in the eggs a little at a time, beating well after each addition.

3 Sift half the flour over the mixture and, using a metal spoon or rubber spatula, gently fold into the mixture. Sift over the remaining flour and fold in until just blended.

4 Divide the mixture between the tins, spreading evenly. Gently smooth the surfaces with the back of a spoon. Bake in the centre of the preheated oven for 20–25 minutes until well risen and golden.

5 Remove and leave to cool before turning out onto a wire rack. Whip the cream with 1 tablespoon of the icing sugar until it forms soft peaks. Fold in the chopped strawberries.

6 Spread one cake layer evenly with the mixture and top with the second cake layer, rounded–side up. Thickly dust the cake with icing sugar and decorate with the reserved strawberries. Carefully slide onto a serving plate and serve.

Ingredients   SERVES 8–10

175 g/6 oz unsalted butter, softened
175 g/6 oz caster sugar
1 tsp vanilla extract
3 large eggs, beaten
175 g/6 oz self-raising flour
150 ml/¼ pint double cream
2 tbsp icing sugar, sifted
225 g/8 oz fresh strawberries, hulled and chopped
few extra strawberries, to decorate

Helpful Hint

For sponge cakes, it is important to achieve the correct consistency of the uncooked mixture. Check it after folding in the flour by tapping a spoonful of the mixture on the side of the bowl. If it drops easily, 'dropping' consistency has been reached. If it is too stiff, fold in a tablespoon of cooled boiled water.

2

4

6

Fat-free Sponge

1   Preheat the oven to 190°C/375°F/Gas Mark 5. Grease two nonstick 18 cm/7 inch sandwich tins, line with nonstick baking parchment, then dust with a mixture of flour and caster sugar.

2   Put the eggs and sugar in a large bowl and stand this over a pan of simmering water. Whisk the eggs and sugar until doubled in volume and the mixture is thick enough to leave a trail on the surface of the batter when the whisk is lifted away.

3   Remove the bowl from the heat and continue whisking for a further 5 minutes until the mixture is cool. Sift half the flour over the mixture and fold in very lightly, using a large metal spoon. Sift in the remaining flour and fold in the same way.

4   Pour the mixture into the tins and tilt them to spread the mixture evenly. Bake for 15–20 minutes until well risen and firm and the cakes are beginning to shrink away from the sides of the tins. Leave to stand for 2 minutes, then turn out to cool on a wire rack.

5   To decorate, whip the cream, if using, and spread half the cream (or crème fraîche or yogurt) over one cake. Swirl 1 tablespoon of the lemon curd into the cream, crème fraîche or yogurt and scatter over half the blueberries. Place the other cake on top and swirl over the remaining cream/yogurt. Swirl over the remaining lemon curd and sprinkle with the remaining berries. Scatter the strips of lemon zest over the top.

Ingredients   SERVES 8

3 medium eggs

175 g/6 oz caster sugar, plus extra for dusting

125 g/4 oz self-raising flour, plus extra for dusting

To decorate:

150 ml/¼ pint low-fat whipping cream, or low-fat crème fraîche or yogurt

2 tbsp lemon curd

125 g/4 oz blueberries

zest of 1 lemon, cut into long thin strips

Coffee & Walnut Muffins

1 Preheat the oven to 180°C/350°F/Gas Mark 4. Grease or line a 12-hole muffin tray with paper cases.

2 Beat the butter and sugar together until light and fluffy. Sift in the flour and baking powder, then add the eggs, golden syrup, vanilla extract and sour cream. Beat together until fluffy, then fold in the nuts.

3 Spoon the batter into the paper cases, filling them about three quarters full. Bake for about 25 minutes until a skewer inserted into the centre comes out clean. Turn out to cool on a wire rack.

4 For the topping, put the cream, sugar, coffee extract and cinnamon in a bowl and whisk until soft peaks form. Swirl over the muffins and top each with a walnut piece. Refrigerate until needed, or keep chilled for 24 hours in an airtight container.

Ingredients   MAKES 2

125 g/4 oz butter, softened
125 g/4 oz soft light brown sugar
150 g/5 oz plain flour
1 tsp baking powder
2 medium eggs
1 tbsp golden syrup
1 tsp vanilla extract
4 tbsp sour cream
40 g/1$^1/_2$ oz walnut pieces, chopped

To decorate:

150 ml/$^1/_4$ pint double cream
1 tbsp golden caster sugar
1 tsp coffee extract
$^1/_2$ tsp ground cinnamon
50 g/2 oz walnut pieces

Easy Chocolate Cake

1 Preheat the oven to 180°C/350°F/Gas Mark 4. Grease two 20.5 cm/8 inch round sandwich tins and line the bases with nonstick baking parchment. Place the chocolate, milk and 75 g/3 oz of the sugar in a heavy-based saucepan. Heat gently until the mixture has melted, then set aside to cool.

2 Place the butter and remaining sugar in a large bowl and whisk with an electric mixer until light and fluffy. Gradually whisk in the eggs, adding 1 teaspoon flour with each addition. Stir in the cooled melted chocolate mixture along with the vanilla extract. Sift in the flour, bicarbonate of soda and cocoa powder, then fold into the mixture until smooth.

3 Spoon the batter into the tins and smooth level. Bake for about 30 minutes until firm to the touch and a skewer inserted into the centre comes out clean. Turn out to cool on a wire rack.

4 To decorate, beat the butter with the icing sugar and 1 tablespoon warm water until light and fluffy, then place half in a piping bag fitted with a star nozzle. Spread half the buttercream over one sponge layer and scatter half the strawberries over it. Top with the other cake and spread the remaining buttercream over the top. Pipe a border of stars around the edge. Decorate with the remaining strawberries and mint sprigs.

Ingredients SERVES 8–10

75 g/3 oz dark chocolate, broken
    into squares
200 ml/7 fl oz milk
250 g/9 oz dark muscovado sugar
75 g/3 oz butter, softened
2 medium eggs, beaten
150 g/5 oz plain flour
$^1/_2$ tsp vanilla extract
1 tsp bicarbonate of soda
25 g/1 oz cocoa powder

For the topping and filling:

125 g/4 oz unsalted butter
225 g/8 oz icing sugar, sifted
175 g/6 oz fresh strawberries, halved
tiny mint sprigs, to decorate

1

3

4

Triple Chocolate Brownies

1 Preheat the oven to 190°C/375°F/Gas Mark 5, 10 minutes before baking. Oil and line a 28 x 18 x 2.5 cm/11 x 7 x 1 inch cake tin with nonstick baking parchment. Place the plain chocolate in a heatproof bowl with the butter set over a saucepan of almost boiling water and stir occasionally until melted. Remove from the heat and leave until just cool, but not beginning to set.

2 Place the caster sugar, eggs, vanilla extract and coffee in a large bowl and beat together until smooth. Gradually beat in the chocolate mixture. Sift the flour into the chocolate mixture. Add the pecans and the white and milk chocolate and gently fold in until mixed thoroughly.

3 Spoon the mixture into the prepared tin and level the top. Bake on the centre shelf of the preheated oven for 45 minutes, or until just firm to the touch in the centre and crusty on top. Leave to cool in the tin, then turn out onto a wire rack. Trim off the crusty edges and cut into 15 squares. Store in an airtight container.

Ingredients   MAKES 5

350 g/12 oz plain dark chocolate, broken into pieces
225 g/8 oz butter, cubed
225 g/8 oz caster sugar
3 large eggs, lightly beaten
1 tsp vanilla extract
2 tbsp very strong black coffee
100 g/3$\frac{1}{2}$ oz self–raising flour
125 g/4 oz pecans, roughly chopped
75 g/3 oz white chocolate, roughly chopped
75 g/3 oz milk chocolate, roughly chopped

Tasty Tip
Take care not to overcook; the outside crust should be crisp and the centre of the brownies moist and gooey.

Very Berry Muffins

1   Preheat the oven to 200˚C/400˚F/Gas Mark 6. Line a deep
    12–hole muffin tray with 10 deep paper cases. Melt the
    butter nd then set aside to cool.

2   Sift the flour, baking powder and bicarbonate of soda into a
    large bowl. Add the sugar and make a well in the centre. Beat
    the egg and milk together in a jug with the orange juice.

3   Pour the milk mixture into the bowl together with the cooled
    butter and the orange zest and beat lightly with a fork until all
    the flour is combined but the mixture is still slightly lumpy.
    Gently fold in the raspberries and cranberries and spoon into
    the paper cases.

4   Bake for about 20 minutes until firm and risen and a skewer
    inserted into the centre comes out clean. Cool on a wire rack.
    Eat warm or cold on the day of baking.

Ingredients   MAKES 10

50 g/2 oz butter
225 g/8 oz plain flour
1 tsp baking powder
$^1/_2$ tsp bicarbonate of soda
65 g/2$^1/_2$ oz golden caster sugar
1 medium egg
175 ml/6 fl oz milk
zest and 1 tbsp juice from
   1 small orange
125 g/4 oz fresh raspberries
50 g/2 oz dried cranberries

Banana Cake

1 Preheat the oven to 190°C/375°F/Gas Mark 5, 10 minutes before baking. Lightly oil and line the base of an 18 cm/7 inch deep round cake tin with greaseproof paper or baking parchment.

2 Mash 2 of the bananas in a small bowl, sprinkle with the lemon juice and a heaped tablespoon of the sugar. Mix together lightly and reserve.

3 Gently heat the remaining sugar and butter or margarine in a small saucepan until the butter has just melted. Pour into a small bowl, then allow to cool slightly. Sift the flour and cinnamon into a large bowl and make a well in the centre.

4 Beat the eggs into the cooled sugar mixture, pour into the well of flour and mix thoroughly.

5 Gently stir in the mashed banana mixture. Pour half of the mixture into the prepared tin. Thinly slice the remaining banana and arrange over the cake mixture.

6 Sprinkle over the chopped walnuts, then cover with the remaining cake mixture. Bake in the oven for 50–55 minutes until well risen and golden brown. Allow to cool in the tin, turn out and sprinkle with the ground cinnamon and caster sugar. Serve hot or cold with a jug of fresh cream for pouring.

Ingredients
CUTS INTO 8 SLICES

3 medium-sized ripe bananas
1 tsp lemon juice
150 g/5 oz soft brown sugar
75 g/3 oz butter or margarine
250 g/9 oz self-raising flour
1 tsp ground cinnamon
3 medium eggs
50 g/2 oz walnuts, chopped
1 tsp each ground cinnamon and
    caster sugar, to decorate
fresh cream, to serve

Helpful Hint

The riper the bananas used in this recipe the better! Look out for reductions in supermarkets and fruit shops as ripe bananas are often sold very cheaply. This cake tastes really delicious the day after it has been made – the sponge solidifies slightly yet does not lose any moisture. Eat within 3–4 days.

Chocolate Fudge Brownies

1 Preheat the oven to 180°C/350°F/Gas Mark 4, 10 minutes before baking. Lightly oil and line a 20.5 cm/8 inch square cake tin with greaseproof paper or baking parchment.

2 Slowly melt the butter and chocolate together in a heatproof bowl set over a sauce-pan of simmering water. Transfer the mixture to a large bowl.

3 Stir in the sugar and vanilla extract, then stir in the eggs. Sift over the flour and fold together well with a metal spoon or rubber spatula. Pour into the prepared tin.

4 Transfer to the preheated oven and bake for 30 minutes until just set. Remove the cooked mixture from the oven and leave to cool in the tin before turning it out onto a wire rack.

5 Sift the icing sugar and cocoa powder into a small bowl and make a well in the centre.

6 Place the butter in the well, then gradually add about 2 tablespoons hot water. Mix to form a smooth spreadable icing.

7 Pour the icing over the cooked mixture. Allow the icing to set before cutting into squares. Serve the brownies when they are cold.

Ingredients   MAKES 16

125 g/4 oz butter
175 g/6 oz plain dark chocolate.
  roughly chopped or broken
225 g/8 oz caster sugar
2 tsp vanilla extract
2 medium eggs, lightly beaten
150 g/5 oz plain flour
175 g/6 oz icing sugar
2 tbsp cocoa powder
15 g/$^1/_2$ oz butter

Food Fact

Chocolate is obtained from the bean of the cacao tree and was introduced to Europe in the 16th century. It is available in many different forms from cocoa powder to couverture, which is the best chocolate to use for cooking as it has a high cocoa butter content and melts very smoothly.

Citrus Cake

1 Preheat the oven to 190°C/375°F/ Gas Mark 5, 10 minutes before baking. Lightly oil and line the base of a round 20.5 cm/8 inch deep cake tin with baking parchment.

2 In a large bowl, cream the sugar and butter or margarine together until light and fluffy. Whisk the eggs together and beat into the creamed mixture a little at a time.

3 Beat in the orange juice with 1 tablespoon of the flour. Sift the remaining flour onto a large plate several times, then, with a metal spoon or rubber spatula, fold into the creamed mixture.

4 Spoon into the prepared cake tin. Stir the finely grated orange zest into the lemon curd and dot randomly across the top of the mixture.

5 Using a fine skewer, swirl the lemon curd through the cake mixture. Bake in the preheated oven for 35 minutes until risen and golden. Allow to cool for 5 minutes in the tin, then turn out carefully onto a wire rack.

6 Sift the icing sugar into a bowl, add the grated lemon zest and juice and stir well to mix. When the cake is cold, cover the top with the icing and serve.

Ingredients

CUTS INTO
6 SLICES

175 g/6 oz golden caster sugar
175 g/6 oz butter or margarine
3 medium eggs
2 tbsp orange juice
175 g/6 oz self-raising flour
finely grated zest of 2 oranges
5 tbsp lemon curd
125 g/4 oz icing sugar
finely grated zest of 1 lemon
1 tbsp freshly squeezed lemon juice

Food Fact

Repeated sifting as in step 3 removes impurities from the flour while adding air to it. Using golden caster sugar gives a richer sweeter taste than normal caster sugar and contrasts particularly well with the citrus flavour in this cake.

Chocolate Nut Brownies

1 Preheat the oven to 180°C/350°F/Gas Mark 4, 10 minutes before baking. Lightly oil and line a 20.5 cm/8 inch square cake tin with greaseproof paper or baking parchment.

2 Combine the butter, sugar and chocolate in a small saucepan and heat gently until the sugar and chocolate have melted, stirring constantly. Reserve and cool slightly.

3 Mix together the peanut butter, eggs and peanuts in a large bowl. Stir in the cooled chocolate mixture. Sift in the flour and fold together with a metal spoon or rubber spatula until combined.

4 Pour into the prepared tin and bake in the preheated oven for about 30 minutes until just firm. Cool for 5 minutes in the tin before turning out onto a wire rack to cool.

5 To make the topping, melt the chocolate in a heatproof bowl over a saucepan of simmering water, making sure that the base of the bowl does not touch the water.

6 Cool slightly, then stir in the sour cream until smooth and glossy. Spread over the brownies, refrigerate until set, then cut into squares. Serve the brownies cold.

Ingredients   MAKES 3

125 g/4 oz butter
150 g/5 oz soft light brown sugar, firmly packed
50 g/2 oz plain dark chocolate, roughly chopped or broken
2 tbsp smooth peanut butter
2 medium eggs
50 g/2 oz unsalted roasted peanuts finely chopped
100 g/3$^1/_2$ oz self-raising flour

For the topping:
125 g/4 oz plain dark chocolate, roughly chopped or broken
50 ml/2 fl oz sour cream

Tasty Tip
For those with a really sweet tooth, replace the plain dark chocolate used for the topping with white chocolate. Buy a good-quality chocolate and take care when melting, as it burns very easily in the microwave.

Chocolate & Coconut Cake

1 Preheat the oven to 180°C/350°F/Gas Mark 4, 10 minutes before baking. Melt the chocolate in a small bowl placed over a saucepan of gently simmering water, ensuring that the base of the bowl does not touch the water. When the chocolate has melted, stir until smooth and allow to cool.

2 Lightly oil and line the bases of two 18 cm/7 inch sandwich tins with greaseproof paper or baking parchment. In a large bowl, beat the butter or margarine and sugar together with a wooden spoon until light and creamy. Beat in the eggs a little at a time, then stir in the melted chocolate.

3 Sift the flour and cocoa powder together and gently fold into the chocolate mixture with a metal spoon or rubber spatula. Add the desiccated coconut and mix lightly. Divide between the two prepared tins and smooth the tops.

4 Bake in the preheated oven for 25–30 minutes until a skewer comes out clean when inserted into the centre of the cake. Allow to cool in the tin for 5 minutes, then turn out, discard the lining paper and leave on a wire rack until cold.

5 Beat together the butter or margarine and creamed coconut until light. Add the icing sugar and mix well. Spread half of the icing onto one cake and press the cakes together. Spread the remaining icing over the top, sprinkle with the coconut and serve.

Ingredients

CUTS INTO
8 SLICES

125 g/4 oz plain dark chocolate roughly chopped
175 g/6 oz butter or margarine
175 g/6 oz caster sugar
3 medium eggs, beaten
175 g/6 oz self-raising flour
1 tbsp cocoa powder
50 g/2 oz desiccated coconut

For the icing:

125 g/4 oz butter or margarine
2 tbsp creamed coconut
225 g/8 oz icing sugar
25 g/1 oz desiccated coconut, lightly toasted

Tasty Tip

Why not experiment with the chocolate in this recipe? For a different taste, try using orange-flavoured dark chocolate or add 1–2 tablespoons rum when melting the chocolate.

Victoria Sponge with Mango & Mascarpone

1 Preheat the oven to 190°C/375°F/Gas Mark 5, 10 minutes before baking. Lightly oil two 18 cm/7 inch sandwich tins and lightly dust with caster sugar and flour, tapping the tins to remove any excess.

2 In a large bowl, cream the butter or margarine and sugar together with a wooden spoon until light and creamy. In another bowl, mix the eggs and vanilla extract together. Sift the flour several times onto a plate. Beat a little egg into the butter and sugar, then a little flour and beat well.

3 Continue adding the flour and eggs alternately, beating after each addition, until the mixture is well mixed and smooth. Divide between the two cake tins, level the surface, then, using the back of a large spoon, make a slight dip in the centre of each cake.

4 Bake in the oven for 25–30 minutes until the centre of the cake springs back when gently pressed with a clean finger. Turn out onto a wire rack and leave the cakes until cold.

5 Beat the icing sugar and mascarpone cheese together, then chop the mango into small cubes. Use half the mascarpone and mango to sandwich the cakes together. Spread the rest of the mascarpone on top, decorate with the remaining mango and serve. Otherwise, lightly cover and store in the refrigerator.

Ingredients
CUTS INTO 8 SLICES

175 g/6 oz caster sugar, plus extra for dusting
175 g/6 oz self-raising flour, plus extra for dusting
175 g/6 oz butter or margarine
3 large eggs
1 tsp vanilla extract
25 g/1 oz icing sugar
250 g/9 oz mascarpone cheese
1 large ripe mango, peeled

Tasty Tip
Mango has been used in this recipe, but 125 g/4 oz mashed strawberries could be used instead. Reserve a few whole strawberries, slice and use to decorate the cake.

1

3

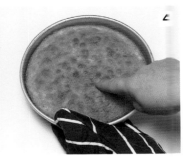

Swiss Roll

1   Preheat the oven to 220°C/425°F/Gas Mark 7, 15 minutes before
    baking. Lightly oil and line the base of a 23 x 33 cm/9 x 13 inch
    Swiss roll tin with a single sheet of greaseproof/baking paper. Sift
    the flour several times; reserve on top of the oven to warm a little.

2   Place a mixing bowl with the eggs, vanilla extract and sugar
    over a saucepan of simmering water, ensuring that the base of
    the bowl is not touching the water. With the saucepan off the
    heat, whisk with an electric hand whisk until the egg mixture
    becomes pale and mousse-like and has increased in volume.
    Remove the basin from the saucepan and continue to whisk
    for a further 2–3 minutes. Sift in the flour and very gently fold
    in using a metal spoon or rubber spatula, trying not to knock
    out the air already whisked in. Pour into the prepared tin, tilting
    to ensure that the mixture is evenly distributed.

3   Bake in the oven for 10–12 minutes until well risen, golden
    brown and the top springs back when touched lightly with a
    clean finger. Sprinkle the toasted chopped hazelnuts over a
    large sheet of greaseproof paper. When the cake has cooled,
    turn out onto the hazelnut-covered paper and trim the edges
    of the cake. Holding an edge of the paper with the short side
    of the cake nearest you, roll the cake up. When fully cold,
    carefully unroll and spread with the jam and then the cream.
    Roll back up and serve. Otherwise, store in the refrigerator and
    eat within 2 days.

Ingredients

CUTS INTO
8 SLICES

75 g/3 oz self-raising flour
3 large eggs
1 tsp vanilla extract
100 g/3½ oz caster sugar
25 g/1 oz hazelnuts, toasted and
    finely chopped
3 tbsp apricot conserve
300 ml/½ pint double cream,
    lightly whipped

Tasty Tip

Any flavour of jam can be used in
this recipe. While apricot jam is
delicious, traditional raspberry or
blackcurrant jam also works very well.
In place of the cream, why not try
buttercream icing or beaten
mascarpone as a filling?

Coffee & Pecan Cake

1 Preheat the oven to 190°C/375°F/Gas Mark 5, 10 minutes before baking. Lightly oil and line the bases of two 18 cm/7 inch sandwich tins with greaseproof paper or baking parchment. Sift the flour and reserve.

2 Beat the butter or margarine and sugar together until light and creamy. Dissolve the coffee in 2 tablespoons hot water and allow to cool.

3 Lightly mix the eggs with the coffee liquid. Gradually beat into the creamed butter and sugar, adding a little of the sifted flour with each addition.

4 Fold in the pecans, then divide the mixture between the prepared tins and bake in the preheated oven for 20–25 minutes until well risen and firm to the touch. Leave to cool in the tins for 5 minutes before turning out and cooling on a wire rack.

5 To make the icing, blend together the coffee and cocoa powder with enough boiling water to make a stiff paste. Beat into the butter and icing sugar.

6 Sandwich the two cakes together using half of the icing. Spread the remaining icing over the top of the cake and decorate with the whole pecans to serve. Store in an airtight container.

Ingredients CUTS INTO 8 SLICES

175 g/6 oz self-raising flour
125 g/4 oz butter or margarine
175 g/6 oz golden caster sugar
1 tbsp instant coffee powder or granules
2 large eggs
50 g/2 oz pecans, roughly chopped

For the icing:
1 tsp instant coffee powder or granules
1 tsp cocoa powder
75 g/3 oz unsalted butter, softened
175 g/6 oz icing sugar, sifted
whole pecans, to decorate

Marble Cake

1   Preheat the oven to 190°C/375°F/Gas Mark 5, 10 minutes before baking. Lightly oil and line the base of a 20.5 cm/8 inch deep round cake tin with greaseproof paper or baking parchment.

2   In a large bowl, cream the butter or margarine and sugar together until light and fluffy. Beat the eggs together. Beat into the mixture a little at a time, beating well after each addition. When all the egg has been added, fold in the flour with a metal spoon or rubber spatula. Divide the mixture equally between 2 bowls. Beat the grated orange zest into one of the bowls with a little of the orange juice. Mix the cocoa powder with the remaining orange juice until smooth, then add to the other bowl and beat well.

3   Spoon the mixture into the tin, in alternate spoonfuls. When all the cake mixture is in the tin, take a skewer and swirl it in the two mixtures. Tap the base of the tin on the work surface to level the mixture. Bake in the oven for 50 minutes, or until cooked and a skewer inserted into the centre of the cake comes out clean. Remove from the oven and leave in the tin for a few minutes before cooling on a wire rack. Discard the lining paper.

4   For the topping, place the orange zest and juice with the granulated sugar in a small saucepan and heat gently until the sugar has dissolved. Bring to the boil and simmer gently for 3–4 minutes until the juice is syrupy. Pour over the cooled cake and serve when cool. Otherwise, store in an airtight tin.

Ingredients
CUTS INTO 8 SLICES

225 g/8 oz butter or margarine
225 g/8 oz caster sugar
4 medium eggs
225 g/8 oz self-raising flour, sifted
finely grated zest and juice of
   1 orange
25 g/1 oz cocoa powder, sifted

For the topping:
zest and juice of 1 orange
1 tbsp granulated sugar

Helpful Hint
This cake has a wonderful combination of rich chocolate and orangey sponge. It is important not to swirl too much in step 3, as the desired effect is to have blocks of different coloured sponge.

All-in-one Chocolate Fudge Cakes

1 Preheat the oven to 180°C/350°F/Gas Mark 4, 10 minutes before baking. Oil and line a 28 x 18 x 2.5 cm/11 x 7 x 1 inch cake tin with nonstick baking parchment.

2 Place the soft brown sugar and butter in a bowl and sift in the flour, cocoa powder, baking powder and salt. Add the eggs and golden syrup, then beat with an electric whisk for 2 minutes, before adding 2 tablespoons warm water and beating for a further 1 minute.

3 Turn the mixture into the prepared tin and level the top with the back of a spoon. Bake on the centre shelf of the preheated oven for 30 minutes, or until firm to the touch. Turn the cake out onto a wire rack and leave to cool before removing the baking parchment.

4 To make the topping, gently heat the sugar and evaporated milk in a saucepan, stirring frequently, until the sugar has dissolved. Bring the mixture to the boil and simmer for 6 minutes, without stirring.

5 Remove the mixture from the heat. Add the chocolate and butter and stir until melted and blended. Pour into a bowl and chill in the refrigerator for 1–2 hours until thickened. Spread the topping over the cake, then sprinkle with the chopped fudge. Cut the cake into 15 squares before serving.

Ingredients
MAKES 15 SQUARES

175 g/6 oz soft dark brown sugar
175 g/6 oz butter, softened
150 g/5 oz self–raising flour
25 g/1 oz cocoa powder
$^1/_2$ tsp baking powder
pinch salt
3 medium eggs, lightly beaten
1 tbsp golden syrup

For the fudge topping:
75 g/3 oz granulated sugar
150 ml/$^1/_4$ pint evaporated milk
175 g/6 oz plain dark chocolate, roughly chopped
40 g/1$^1/_2$ oz unsalted butter, softened
125 g/4 oz soft fudge sweets, finely chopped

Tasty Tip
Use a mixture of fudge sweets for the topping on this cake, including chocolate, vanilla and toffee flavours.

Index